DATE DUE

MAZZINI

By the same author

THE FRENCH REVOLUTION
1788-1792

MAZZINI

by

GAETANO SALVEMINI

Translated from the Italian by

I. M. RAWSON

STANFORD UNIVERSITY PRESS
STANFORD, CALIFORNIA

[redacted]

FIRST PUBLISHED 1957

LIBRARY OF CONGRESS CATALOG CARD NO.
57-7972

PRINTED IN GREAT BRITAIN IN THE CITY OF OXFORD
AT THE ALDEN PRESS
BOUND BY A. W. BAIN & CO. LTD., LONDON

CONTENTS

PART ONE

MAZZINI'S TEACHING

PART TWO

THE MAN OF ACTION

CONTENTS

PREFACE

In 1905, when this book first appeared, Mazzinian studies were in their infancy. Apart from the *Life* by Bolton King and Cantimori's admirable *Saggio sull' idealismo di Giuseppe Mazzini* no serious work on Mazzini existed. Since that time much valuable research has been done. Among the best books published recently are those of Alessandro Levi on *La filosofia politica di Giuseppe Mazzini* (Zanichelli, Bologna, 1917, 2nd edition 1923); Manucci's *Giuseppe Mazzini e la prima fase del suo pensiero letterario* (Casa Editrice Risorgimento, Milan, 1919); Luzio's revealing volumes *La madre di Mazzini* (1919), *Mazzini carbonaro* (1920), and *Carlo Alberto e Mazzini* (1923), all published by Bocca, of Turin; and Rodolfo Mondolfo's fine study 'Mazzini e Marx' in the volume entitled *Sulle orme di Marx* (Cappelli, Rocca di San Casciano, 1924). Furthermore we now have the national edition of Mazzini's works and Letters, and his correspondence with a family of English friends, edited by Mrs. Richards.

After so much labour by others and the passing of twenty years, I am conscious of a sense of dissatisfaction on re-reading this book of mine written in what seems another age. Not that there are errors of fact to be put right, or that I feel prompted to modify the conclusions I then reached. But there is a great deal more that I would like to add in order to make the book fully worthy of its subject. The Mazzini here depicted, especially in the first part, is the inflexible Mazzini whose doctrine has achieved its final form. The real and more fascinating Mazzini is missing: the Mazzini who, throughout the tragic experiences of his youth, is still seeking himself; then the Mazzini who forces himself, in the desolation of defeat, to re-elaborate his own faith; and finally the Mazzini who gains contact once more with reality in his years of maturity, strengthened but at the same time misled by preconceptions irrevocably fixed, and, contending desperately with a hostile world, succeeds in imposing his own political ideal of a united Italy upon it, only to see all his religious and social philosophy come to nothing. I do not know whether I shall ever have time or strength to carry out the design that I have in mind. But this at least I know: that if I could have my way with this early work of mine, I would re-write it from beginning to end.

In the meantime the book is always in demand, and may well continue to serve the purpose of those who wish to find in a condensed form all that is essential to Mazzini's thought; even if the best of Mazzini, his life, is absent from its pages.

Florence, February 1925 G. Salvemini

NOTE
TO THE ENGLISH EDITION

THIRTY more years have passed — years, for me, of exile, political strife and war — and have left me without hope of re-writing this book along the lines indicated in the foregoing Preface. Nevertheless, it seems to me that its analysis of Mazzini's thought and political action may still be of use, not only to students of the Italian Risorgimento, but to those interested in the development of nineteenth-century social ideas; indeed, that it may have gained in perspective, in the light of recent events. For this English edition I have made a few alterations in the text and have inserted some additional material. In the main, however, the book stands in its original form.

Sorrento, 1956 G. S.

PART ONE

MAZZINI'S TEACHING

PROLOGUE

THE first half of the nineteenth century was dominated in Europe by a widespread movement of reaction against the classical, materialist and agnostic thought of the preceding century. It was the golden age of idealism, romanticism and sentimentalism. The conservative forces, having recovered from the dismay engendered by the French Revolution, rallied round the absolute monarchies and the Church, and countered Voltaire's anti-clericalism and the materialism of Diderot, which they maintained had given rise to the revolutionary upheaval, with the Catholic, monarchical and feudal mysticism of Joseph de Maistre. Their more extreme democratic opponents, on the other hand, blamed the Revolution and its theorists for having brought about the substitution of an aristocracy of birth by one of wealth; they rejected the utilitarianism of liberal economics, maintained that materialism was a sorry philosophy and inimical to a well-regulated social order, endeavoured to find a religious basis for democracy, and made war on the Catholic Church not in the name of philosophic rationalism but in that of a new mysticism claiming to be more in conformity with the humane spirit of the Gospels. Even among the liberal middle classes, which had emerged triumphant from the Revolution, there were very few who dared to praise as a whole the wonderful intellectual work of the eighteenth century, which nevertheless had paved the way for the Revolution and for the acceptance of the bourgeois social order: the majority took refuge in a cautious opportunism, confining themselves to taking over from the eighteenth century its hostility towards the Jesuits, Montesquieu's constitutional principles, the defence of private property from the encroachments of State control, and other ideas of a similar sort that were far from dangerous and indeed conservative in their nature. Italy, during this time, produced Manzoni's *Inni Sacri*, Silvio Pellico's *Doveri degli uomini* and the philosophical writings of Rosmini and Gioberti; Romagnosi and Melchiorre Gioia, if not actually abused, were forgotten; Giuseppe Ferrari was regarded as an eccentric and misguided thinker; while Carlo Cattaneo remained apart from the main stream of history and thought.

Giuseppe Mazzini's intellectual development, from his fifteenth to his thirtieth year, took place in this atmosphere of romanticism. After a brief period of youthful unbelief, he, too, was caught up for life by the wave of mysticism, which carried all before it and seemed destined to sweep into oblivion the prodigious intellectual achievements of the eighteenth century.

I

THE CRITERION OF TRUTH

TRUTH, according to Mazzini, is to be sought among 'the secrets of an intuition that defies analysis', 'in the rapid, intense concentration of every faculty upon a given point', 'in the most secret aspirations of the soul' and in those 'supreme moments of deep feeling and reverence which the heart knows after having purified itself like a sanctuary of every unworthy passion, of every guilty desire and of all idolatrous superstition'.

The principles revealed to us by individual intuition cannot, however, be considered reliable until their measure has been taken by the 'common consent of humanity'. When the promptings of our inmost spirit coincide with the 'universal tradition', in other words, with what has been affirmed as true not by a single school or religion, nor by a single epoch, but by every school, religion and epoch, then, and then only, can we be sure of standing possessed of the truth.[1] 'Tradition and moral judgment are and ever will be the wings

[1] See Bolton King, *Mazzini*; Cantimori, *Saggio sull'idealismo di Giuseppe Mazzini*, Faenza, Montanari, 1904, pp. 188-90; Calabrò, *La dottrina religioso-sociale nelle opere di Giuseppe Mazzini: La religione dell'avvenire, la teorica della rivoluzione*, Palermo, Reber, 1912, pp. 51 et seqq.

by which human nature can soar to reach the truth'; 'truth is to be found wherever tradition, the life of those who have gone before us, and the call of our own conscience are in agreement; wherever they are found in opposition to one another, lies error'.[1]

In this way Mazzini sought to reconcile traditionalism, which found truth in what had been believed *semper, ubique ab omnibus*, with romanticism, which held truth to be something revealed to the individual spirit in moments of exaltation, without any guidance from logical laws. But from Mazzini's thought in all its aspects it is clear that, for him, intuition is the primary and indeed the greatest source of truth; the study of tradition is only of secondary importance, to be regarded rather as a means of investigation than of conquest.

As soon as he is forced to set out the basic principles of his system, Mazzini always ends by relegating the universal assent of mankind into the second place, and makes his appeal only to 'the intuition of the loving soul in all the dignity of life', to the '*all but inexplicable* moments of inspiration': and speaks of 'a kind of compulsion, *inexplicable* to myself, that directs all my actions, and that — being in the nature of religious stimulus, to which, when I feel it, it seems a crime not to give way — will always remain a secret from every-

[1] Elsewhere Mazzini writes that the sole criterion of certainty is Morality. The contradiction between this assertion and the statements quoted above can be reconciled if it is borne in mind that by Morality Mazzini means, in this case, the moral principles that are revealed to us directly or deduced by reason from what is conveyed by intuition and supported by tradition.

one else, since I know not how to explain it and others would not understand it'.[1] 'Not the mind, but the heart, the instinctive sense of things invisible, the sense of the divine, combine in me to preserve my beliefs.' 'Do not reply to me,' he wrote to a friend in 1833: 'I can only give you some slight indication of my ideas; but they are deeply-rooted in me, they have entered into my very being, into my soul; and I believe that no human intelligence could tear them from me without destroying all the framework of my inner life.'

The reasoning processes with which Nature has endowed man and through the use of which the intellectual expects to discover truth, have only a subordinate function in Mazzini's system. Reason helps us to deduct 'second-grade truths' from the fundamental, intuitive truths, from the 'foundations of belief'; but 'it is not, nor can it ever be, the supreme criterion of certainty'. 'Without *method*, scientific knowledge — in all its truth, fertility and greatness — is impossible; and method can only be acquired through a religious and philosophical approach' which is revealed by intuition, in moments of ecstatic exaltation. That kind of knowledge 'which today is called Free Thought and Reason', is but an 'arid, desiccated and sorry travesty of true knowledge'.[2]

[1] Cantimori, '*Mazzini e la rinascenza religiosa del suo secolo*', in the volume entitled *Mazzini*, Genoa, Fed. Chiesa, 1906, p. 8.

[2] Mazzini's last years, in particular, were spent in a continual battle against atheism, materialism and free thought. This did not prevent the centenary of his birth from being celebrated in Rome in 1905 by an international Congress of Free Thought.

2

FOUNDATIONS OF BELIEF

THE 'foundations of belief', as revealed by intuition and confirmed by tradition, are the following:

I. *The existence of God.* 'Father, Intellect and Love, Creator and educator of humanity': the truth of this 'primary principle' has no need to be demonstrated; 'any attempt to do so would be blasphemy; any denial, madness'.

II. *The unity of the human race.* Mankind 'is a collective entity, in which every generation is bound up with those that preceded and will follow it; in which the existence of each individual is so closely linked with those of others that his own is multiplied. The life of mankind is continual and its faculties are the sum of all those individual faculties that have been exercised for perhaps four hundred centuries. It is a being that learns, through the faults and errors of individuals, continually to improve in wisdom and morality, and in whose development God has written, and writes in every epoch, a line of his own law'.

III. *The constant, unlimited progress of mankind.* This is 'the law that God has given to Life', 'the supreme formula of the creative activity, omnipotent and universal as life itself', 'revealed indisputably by historical tradition and by the aspirations of the soul'.

IV. *Association*. 'General co-operation and the harmony of work' 'must progressively replace individual effort'. This is 'the way of progress'; 'the only means of progress'; 'the mainspring of the world, the only means of regeneration given to the human family'.[1]

[1] When Mazzini tries to give a systematic explanation of his faith he never makes any clear distinction between fundamental and secondary principles. But the ideas set forth above are always present: they are the presuppositions of every one of Mazzini's theories and are to be found in all his writings. It seems justifiable therefore to separate them from the rest and to regard them as basic to the whole system.

3

THE EDUCATION OF MANKIND

MANKIND, therefore, progresses towards the goal for which God has created it, in other words, towards 'the full, free and well-regulated development of all its faculties', 'according to a design laid down by Providence for its education'. 'God directs human affairs.' 'God the Father, by means of a slow but continual religious education, guides mankind towards a better life, in which our individual life too finds improvement.'

The religious education of mankind occurs through successive and progressive revelations. 'The Ideal is external to ourselves and supreme over us; it is not creation, it is discovered by the intellect.' 'Revelation descends continually from God to us, to be the education of the human race.' 'The generations, as daughters of God and sisters in their faculties and tendencies, transmit one to another — each more or less splendid according to its time and its achievements — the spark of life that is derived from Him, nourished and fertilized by His spirit.' 'From one form of work to another, from one belief to another, mankind gradually attains to a clearer understanding of its own life and its own mission, of God and of His law.'

Each stage of education constitutes a different period in the history of mankind. 'Every epoch reveals a fragment of the Ideal, a line of the divine concept,' and 'all are characterized and defined by a religion'. 'Speaking historically, I know of no single great conquest made by the human spirit, no important step forward in the perfecting of human society, that has not had its roots in a strong religious faith.' 'The social structure of the world about us is simply a manifestation of the inner man, of the moral and intellectual condition of humanity in a given period, and in particular of his faith.' 'The idea of society only follows upon that of religion.' 'The history of mankind is the history of the progressive religion of mankind.'

'Every religion holds out to men, as an end in itself, a fragment of this educative idea: a fragment, limited, and contained within symbols, of the eternal Truth.' When the religious principle, having animated a period of human history, 'has attained to its full development, it becomes identified with the progress of civilization and of customs'; and a new phase of history then begins, with the revelation of a new dogma in which are gathered up the riches of all the conquests made in the preceding periods, completed and made perfect through a new victory of the spirit.

The new dogma is 'generally first glimpsed by philosophy, or prepared by the progress of knowledge, or, more often, by the social conditions of a people or of several peoples'; but 'it conquers the soul of the multitude, and is transformed into an axiom of religion' only when 'it is embodied in the life of one or more individuals privileged in their wisdom and love'. Then strikes the hour of the new Advent. 'God puts into a people's heart, or into the mind of a man strong in love and genius, a new belief, greater and more fertile than that which is dying out: the centre of faith moves a stage forward and only the men who take their stand around it will form the party of the future.' Men of genius are 'the angels of God upon earth', 'milestones on the way trodden by mankind', 'the priests of its religion'. 'The ways of Genius are secret, like those of God, by whom it is inspired.'

When, therefore, owing to the preparatory work of men of genius, the new principle has been fully elaborated 'in the sphere of spiritual activity', there generally occurs 'a great crisis, an insurrection, a spontaneous, collective and abnormal uprising of the multitude': since 'the secret of the age, like the Law of Mount Sinai, cannot be revealed except from the midst of the storm'. Then the old authorities are overthrown and new powers arise whose mission it is to unfold 'slowly, progressively and in a normal manner' all the practical consequences of the principle that has been conquered intellectually. At the same time — while, step by step, the application of the religious principle that has triumphed is being carried out — 'a new *idea* and a new goal presents itself to the mind; a new concept of life arises to consecrate this idea; the former religion, having fulfilled its own mission, disappears, leaving behind it — set free for ever from forms and symbols — immortal, immutable, *incognita*, the residue of Truth that it contained'; and the elaboration of a new faith begins.

The new religious principle always stands in this relation to the old, the practical achievements of which are a necessary starting-point for the conquests that will result from the new one. 'If this were not so, Progress could only operate by leaps and bounds. The human intellect would remain inert throughout the period of practical application. And all practical genius, once the work of application was done with, would in its turn have to remain inert, until the intellectual evolution of the new idea was completed. The periods of human progress, interrupted by these periods of inertia, would have need of some impulse, of some higher power of initiative, to link them up. This is the theory of direct, immediate revelation, which we reject as false, and contrary to all that we divine to be of the nature of God.'

4

RELIGIONS OF THE PAST

IN the course of this unbroken chain of progressive revelation 'the first men were made aware of God; but being unaccustomed to detach themselves from the sphere of objects known through the senses, they turned Him into one of these: into the tree that they had seen struck by lightning, into the rock near which they had raised their tent, into the first beast upon which their eyes happened to light'; and thus fetishism began.

The ancient religions of the East, having passed beyond fetishism, proclaimed the idea of God, but neglected Man: 'upon the one hand there was an immense, inscrutable force, and on the other immense weakness, unknowing, passive. Man lay crushed, a slave, the plaything of an inexorable Fate, or of the caprice of the powers of Nature made divine'.

Polytheistic religions freed man from oppressive pantheism, and asserted the freedom of the individual; but they accepted inequality and slavery as belonging to the natural order of things.

Finally came Christianity, which completed the work begun by polytheism, affirming the equality of all classes and all peoples before the one God, Father of all, and bringing to perfection the principles of individuality: since equality is the liberty of all men.

The principle of individuality, revealed by polytheism and perfected by Christianity, 'achieved its highest expression and extended the application of its theories to every branch of human knowledge, manifesting its spirit in religion and philosophy, in morals and politics, in literature and political economy' during the eighteenth century. The eighteenth century acclaimed Liberty and asserted that 'without equality liberty does not exist; all men are equal'. And since, to the development of the individual — 'free, active, sacred, inviolable, as he is called to be' — a multitude of obstacles were raised, the eighteenth century created the theory of human rights, upholding it in opposition to the despotism of the former powers; 'it rejected the inertia of the past, rejected feudalism, aristocracy, monarchy; it rejected Catholic dogma, the dogma of absolute passivity, which poisoned the springs of liberty and made tyranny supreme'; and thus made the great Revolution.

The problem of individual freedom completed by equality having been surmounted, the period that was drawing to a close 'had as its mission that of developing the individual man, the human *ego*, from every point of view. It had as its programme *God and Man*, and it fulfilled it'.[1]

[1] Almost all these ideas on the law of progress, collective humanity, successive and progressive revelation, men of genius, the eighteenth century, and the French Revolution, are in origin those of Saint-Simon, and are to be found in the journals and propagandist writings of his disciples between 1825 and 1835. Of these, in

And now new problems began to disturb men's minds. Once liberty and equality were won, the question arose of the aim of liberty. 'And what of equality? The free man is merely an *active force* ready to operate. In what way should this force operate? At random, in any direction? This is not *life*, but rather a succession of actions, of phenomena, of spurts of unrestrained energy, without reference to one another and without continuity; its name is anarchy. The liberty of one man will inevitably clash with that of another: we should have endless strife between individuals, entailing a useless dispersal of strength and of the productive faculty that lies within us and should be sacred. Freedom for all, without a law in common to direct it, leads to warfare for all; and the greater the equality of the combatants the more savage will this warfare be.'

The doctrine of individual rights 'has overturned, destroyed or undermined all forms of despotism', religious, political, intellectual or economic: 'It has conquered freedom of belief, freedom of the press, commercial freedom and political guarantees; no-one can now tear up the splendid page written by this school of thought in the history of mankind.' But 'strict examination shows us that the doctrine of human

particular, the works of Pierre Leroux and Jean Reynaud had a deep influence on Mazzini during what were for him the formative years from 1830 to 1835, when his thought was taking on its final shape. See Pezzani, *La pluralité des existences de l'âme*, Paris, Lib. Acad. Didier et Cie, 1872, pp. 338-9; Weill, *L'école saint-simonienne*, Paris, Alcan, 1896, pp. 27 et seqq., 158, 463; Charléty, *Histoire du saint-simonisme*, Paris, Hachette, 1896, pp. 17, 43-50, 66, 76, 85, 129; Thomas, *Pierre Leroux*, Paris, Alcan, 1904, pp. 39 et seqq., 77; Isambert, *Les idées socialistes en France de 1815 à 1848*, Paris, Alcan, 1905, pp. 68, 108, 237, 286.

rights is, in essence, only a great and sacred protest in the face of every tyrant who would trample upon freedom. Its value is merely negative. Strong in destruction, it is powerless to build up. It can break fetters, but cannot forge the bonds of harmonious work and love'. 'The doctrine of rights does not comprise the necessity of progress; it admits it as a simple fact. The exercise of rights being necessarily optional, progress is left to the mercy of an unregulated and undirected freedom.' 'The rights of individuals or of different social orders, if not harmonized and guided by a common faith in a divine moral law, must lead sooner or later to a reciprocal clash of interests; and all defence of injured rights assumes an aspect of warfare and revenge.'

5

DISCORD IS EVERYWHERE

IT follows that free men, left to themselves, guided by the theory of human rights and mindful only of their own advantage, think merely of overcoming competitive and opposing interests. 'Discord exists everywhere. We have religions that are anathema to one another, powers that thrive upon war, strife between class and class and hostility between political parties.'

States, 'their boundaries laid down by kings or by treaties concluded between privileged families', have no political aims other than the aggrandizement of the reigning dynasties and 'the weakening, in their interest, of all the rest'. 'Treaties are only transactions conceded to necessity; peace is but a truce; the balance of power is an attempt on the part of perennial suspicion and hostility to guard against possible future enemies.' The best way so far evolved by governments of avoiding conflict is the principle of *non-intervention*: 'an abject, cowardly doctrine; atheism transported into international life, the deification of self-interest'. It removes 'one of the most potent impulses towards progress, which, as history teaches us, is almost always fulfilled through acts of intervention'.[1]

Within the confines of each State there is 'an absurd divorce' between the civil authorities and the ecclesiastical hierarchy. They struggle against one another, 'each groping, alone and suspicious, in the dark; watching the other's death agony, in fear and anger'.

In addition to the conflict between Church and State, there is conflict everywhere between capital and labour. 'The capitalist class, which owns the soil and keeps in its own hands all the implements of labour',[2] allots and distributes work as and when it pleases, since the capitalist 'alone is master, and able to promote, drive and direct production towards his own ends'. The working-class, on the other hand, forced to choose between selling its labour day by day or dying of hunger, 'cannot afford to wait, and is therefore forced to accept; it can only submit, and it does so'. Wages therefore are determined by the relationship that exists between the work offered and the work required, in other words, 'between the working population and capitalism'; and since the population 'tends in general to increase in a greater degree than capital increases',

[1] These theories, too, and those that follow on the sterility of art and the necessity of a new religion, are Saint-Simonist in origin. See Weill, op. cit., pp. 3, 29 et seqq.; Charléty, op. cit., pp. 7-12, 29, 40-1, 129, 142, 457; Thomas, op. cit., pp. 39-40, 46-8, 168 et seqq.; Isambert, op. cit., pp. 101 et seqq., and 284.

[2] This is the famous iron law of capital and wages, which is to be found in writings previous to those of Lassalle, who gave it the name (Fournière, p. 362, Isambert, Lassalle, p. 165): but it seems that Mazzini did not accept it with all its implications. In the *Doveri degli uomini*, after describing the wretched conditions of the working-class and the causes of such conditions, he adds: 'Nevertheless, there is progress in the state of the class to which you belong.' All Mazzini's social theories are imbued as Bolton King rightly observes, with the greatest optimism.

wages tend to fall and the profits of capital to rise. At every attempt by the people to improve their own lot, 'Society replies with cavalry charges and machine-gun fire'. Thus the very principles of individual rights become inapplicable, since for most men, equality is an abstraction and liberty an empty word.

Selfish individualism has even disrupted family life. 'The family, which is a symbol of the way in which God's unceasing work is accomplished in the universe and the germ of society, has become perverted into a denial of all vocation and social duty; male and female have obliterated man and woman.' 'Love, the most holy thing that God has given to man in promise of a fuller life, has become, under the harpy's claws of this profane century, a foulness of the senses, a febrile urge, a brutish instinct, *egoisme à deux personnes*, a jealous passion compounded of pride and the thirst for sensual gratification, which restricts the sphere of our activity and makes us forget our duty towards our country and mankind.' 'Half the human family, that half from which we seek inspiration and comfort and to which we confide the early education of our children, is by a curious inconsistency held to be inferior from the civil, political and social point of view, and is excluded from the unity of the human family.'

'Poets and men of letters are isolated from the rest of the nation and lack any general, overriding sense of their own mission; they are listened to only by a restricted public of other writers, by their wealthy patrons and by academies.' 'For this reason literature has no purpose, no banner, no awareness of the future: it does not reveal to us the things of heaven and earth, the mysteries of this life, or the fate of mankind.' 'Poetry in England died with Byron; in Germany, with Goethe. In France it is becoming extinguished in scepticism and despair. In Italy it sleeps the sleep of Michelangelo's Night.' Music 'is a sterile combination of sounds, without meaning, without unity, without moral ideas'. 'Pedantry and venality have reduced Art to a mechanical and servile exercise, a diversion for the satiated rich.'

What is the cause of so much evil?

'The absence of religious thought.' 'Society as it exists today lacks an active, common faith.' Christianity, as an individualistic religion, 'ignores collective humanity, the Law of Progress by which we are ruled and the historical tradition that reveals this Law and teaches us how it works; it ignores the bonds that exist between every generation, past, present and future, the unity of heaven and earth, the ideal and the real, the infinite and the finite'. Christianity, having completed its great divine and historical mission by instilling into men's minds the principle that all human souls are equal and all men are children of one Father, has nothing new or progressive to teach: 'It does not create, it does not determine or direct men's actions nor does it arouse the will to sacrifice; it does not gather up the various branches of human activity into an harmonious whole.' 'Science', wrote Mazzini in 1870, addressing the Members of the Vatican Council, 'goes forward, regardless of your doctrines, caring nothing for your denunciations and your Councils, tearing up, with every new discovery, a page of the Book that you declare infallible. Art, lost in the void, turns at times to pagan ideals, or gropes after religious inspiration of a kind different from yours, or, as though despairing of finding any other God, worships itself; but it stands ever apart from the Christian faith, always unresponsive to the concept that in past centuries inspired your architects and painters. Governments, in the exercise of their powers, deny you. Those men amongst you who are most outstanding in their intellect or eloquence, leave you one by one. None of the great advances made in our century has been prompted by you or consecrated by your approval. Immobile sphinxes in a vast desert, you remain today gazing passively at the shadow of times past.' Christian dogma no longer corresponds to the stage of education which, by the design of Providence, men have now reached. For this reason 'the Christian faith is dying out among the peoples of the world': 'mind and heart, tradition and conscience, turn from it'.

And with it, Christian morality, cut off from its origins and from divine sanction, and so rendered sterile, is dying too: 'No moral system can remain active and fertile amongst men if it has no heaven and no dogma to support it.' Catholicism[1] has been impotent for six hundred years; it has deserted all Christ's

[1] Mazzini never makes any clear distinction between Christianity and Roman Catholicism.

precepts, it has fornicated with the great ones of this earth, it has substituted the idolatry of empty forms for the Spirit of Religion, and it has been discredited by the immorality of its prominent men. It lays down the negation of progress as a condition of its own life. 'The Papacy dies — most sorry of deaths — uttering maledictions.' It is 'inaccessible to any attempt to reinfuse life into its veins; a travesty of religion and an eternal source of corruption and immorality amongst the nations'. Protestantism has attempted 'the impossible task of leading a religion back to its beginnings, in denial of Progress': it has only suceeded in destroying any common faith by upholding the principle of free investigation, and 'today is dying, dismembered, as an endless number of sects and lesser churches multiply within its breast'.

Whilst the old faith is in its last throes, a new one has not as yet revealed itself; and in this 'transition period between one faith and another, wherein all unity of aim or sense of a common doctrine and a true philosophic system are lost', the intellect can only contribute negation and anarchy. Thus materialism triumphs; it poisons the soul with egoism and cowardice; it reduces life to the search for happiness, that is, for the happiness or pleasure of a day or an hour, procured by gold or by the satisfaction of ignoble and deceptive sensual passions. It makes the individual the centre and the object of every endeavour, is destructive of social life and the sense of collective brotherhood, corrupts the sacred conception of love by transforming it into lust, and the strict standards of our forefathers into shameless licence; it removes woman from the social order, replacing her by the female; and renders poetry and literature impossible.

Meanwhile, an irrepressible restlessness disturbs men's minds: 'a ferment of potentialities that know not how to express themselves in action; a striving after the unknown, that becomes spent without giving rise to positive conquests'.

6

THE NEW REVELATION

BUT 'all anarchy is temporary, and cannot exceed certain limits. It is always the sign of an intermediate period between one epoch and another, between one belief and another'. The human race cannot exist without a faith: 'It has need of an answer to its doubts, and thirsts to know what lies before it. It must be told from whence it comes and whither it is going.' The religious concept 'constitutes a belief in an origin common to us all and puts before us the principle of a common future. It unites all our active faculties in one single centre, from which they turn continually towards that future, and it directs all the forces that lie latent in the human spirit towards attaining it. It leaves its imprint upon every aspect of life, on even the least important of our actions; its blessing lies upon the cradle and the grave; it raises up and purifies the individual; causes the springs of egoism to run dry by changing and directing man's activities outwards instead of inwards: and in creating for man that theory of *duty* which is the parent of sacrifice, it has inspired, and ever will inspire, great and noble deeds'.[1]

[1] From *Fede e avvenire*, 1835, of which Mazzini wrote in 1845 that he considered it the best of his works.

Such an attitude, which 'forces mankind to translate *thought* into *action*, and to bring practical life into harmony with the moral concept' — an attitude which is 'the essence of every religion' — 'is unknown to scientific learning'. 'Philosophy, which proudly claims to be knowledge of life, can only assure the death of one religion and prepare the way for another: it has never done more than this. But when it has thoroughly dissected, analysed and anatomized, it will find itself deprived of that breath of life which, by renewing and enlarging the scope of morality, points out where men's duty lies and urges them to action.'

When the old faith has worn itself out, a new and more perfect one will spring from it, bringing a new and more perfect form of human life. 'We shall have a new heaven and a new earth.' 'The old generation will die, perhaps, in anarchy; but the next will grow up in the search for faith, and will not die before having reconquered it.' 'No, God Eternal! Thy Word is not yet fulfilled. Thy Thought, the thought of the world, is not yet wholly revealed. Yet it incessantly creates, and for many centuries beyond the reach of human calculation it will continue to create. Those already traversed have revealed only a few fragments of it to us. Our mission is not ended.'

In contrast with the Christian Church, which, its mission being that of the triumph of human individuality, had a single precursor, John the Baptist, the new Church destined to spread the religion of collective humanity will have a new collective precursor: that is, an association of precursors and apostles: 'A group of men of powerful intelligence and of proved morality.' And whereas, in the fullness of time, a single individual, Jesus Christ, came to initiate the era that we have just passed through, the initiator of the new social era will be a collective body: 'The Messiah will be a whole people, free, great and bound together by a single thought and a single love', which will owe allegiance only to God in Heaven and mankind on earth. 'When the time is ripe, God inspires in the people that has suffered most and has kept its own faith intact, the will and the courage to conquer or to die for all the rest. This is the initiator-people. It takes up arms and fights: whether it triumphs or dies, from its ashes or its crown of victory the Word of the Epoch will be evolved, and the world will be saved.'

The Messiah-people 'will arise in all the strength of insurrection' and will convene 'a Council of Mankind', a convention of 'the wisest and most virtuous of those who believe in the eternal things, in the mission of God's children upon earth and in the victory of progressive Truth, brought together to inquire religiously into the spirit of this collective humanity, and to ask of the prescient peoples, still uncertain of themselves and of the future: *What part of the old faith is dead in your hearts? What part of the future begins to live in you?* In this Council, the minds of all, brought to the highest pitch of spiritual power by the spectacle of a people of believers, by the contemplation of human nature moved to extraordinary activity and with all its faculties in agreement' — in a moment, in other words, of *intuition* — will receive the new revelation, as the Pentecostal gathering received it. 'The Spirit of God can only descend upon the gathered multitudes. It is for them to say what they believe or do not believe.' 'The Council will elaborate a Declaration not of rights but of principles';[1] and thus the 'great Church' will arise, 'the humanitarian Catholicism', 'the union of believers', in which 'Israelites, Mahometans, Buddhists and all those who in eighteen centuries of striving have not been able to embrace a universal religion, can finally feel themselves brothers'.

[1] For Mazzini *rights* equal *interests*, and *principles*, *duties*.

7

THE NEW DOGMA

'GOD has not given me, nor will He ever give me, strength to be the apostle of this new religion; but I know that it will come.' Mazzini was convinced that the basic dogma of the future faith would be provided by those ideas of God, Progress, Collective Humanity and Association upon which he founded his system. From these ideas the theology and moral principles of the new faith can be deduced.

Christian theology, ignoring the continual progress of the human race, believes in a God Who created the world and then rested, to intervene only now and again in the natural order of things by means of miracles to bestow some particular benefit on man. It regards human ignorance as a permanent fact, and epitomizes the history of humanity in a series of mysteries: the Fall owing to Original Sin, Redemption by means of the Incarnation of the Son of God, eternal salvation or perdition of the individual soul according to predestination, and the Resurrection of the Body. It also affirms the existence between God and Man of a hierarchy of divine beings whose nature is immutable and in essence different from that of men; and so creates a celestial aristocracy of angels inaccessible to mankind.

The dogma of progress, on the other hand, imposes a belief in God as the inexhaustible source of life: creation is continuous, according to a process of amelioration that God, the perfect Being, cannot disturb by any miraculous intervention, since this would betray some initial defect in wisdom or judgment on His part; whereas, every one of His actions must necessarily be identical with Truth and Righteousness. Mysteries do not exist for the human mind, which advances always in the conquest of eternal truth: only the unknown exists, to be revealed to us step by step. Mankind did not set forth on its predestined course from a state of perfection and then experience Error and the Fall, thus violating the law of progress; it started from primitive imperfection, which, little by little, it corrects owing to the capacity for progress with which the Creator has endowed all His creatures. There is no need, therefore, for Redemption by means of the Incarnation and Passion of the Son of God, at a given historical moment; for the redemption of mankind from its original intellectual and moral imperfection is continually taking place. 'Humanity is the living Word of God. It is quickened by the Spirit of God, which is manifested in it ever more clearly, from epoch to epoch. The incarnation of God in mankind occurs successively in noble deeds that show forth the universal life, in great intellects that are sanctified by virtue, and in the high aspirations of the individual consciousness.' Christian dogma humanizes God: the dogma of progress tends, slowly and progressively to make man divine. 'In Christ we do not lose the man born of woman in the God; we love him as a brother who is better than we are. We do not adore him and fear him as the inexorable judge and ruler of the future.'

The new faith will accept Christianity's doctrine of the immortality of the soul, 'which is simply the law of progress applied to life as manifested in the individual'. 'Death does not exist, it cannot even be conceived of: life is life, it is immortality. If it is immortality, it must obey the law of life, which is progress.' And it is as a consequence of the law of gradual progress that the new faith denies the possibility of an immediate passing of the soul from its life on earth to eternal beatitude: human life is too far from the ideal of perfection for such virtue as we are capable of on earth to qualify us for the heights that lead to God. It also denies eternal punishment, since this prevents any rehabilitation or future progress for the soul, and by it 'the divine element that lives in every soul' would be killed: 'a blasphemy towards God, who cannot kill himself in the creature he has created'.

The new faith will replace the dogma of predestination for an elect few by the dogma of salvation for all; and the dogma of the Resurrection by the transformation of men's bodies through 'an indefinite series of reincarnations of the soul, from life to life, from world to world, each of which represents an improvement on the preceding one'. 'This life of ours is only an episode in the life of the soul.' 'It is an intermediate step, a step in the ladder that leads to God.' 'We approach God through a series of lives each one more serene than the last, and less subject to the conflicts and crises of this world. It is in our power to traverse these lives more quickly and to reach the pure souls that have preceded us, raising ourselves up with all our strength by means of virtue, love and sacrifice.' 'If we have not known how to rise above it, we can repeat the stage that we have already done, but we cannot go backwards or perish spiritually.' The journey from one kind of existence to the next 'is made as though round an enormous pyramid, in such a way that those who have reached a certain height can begin to discern the path they have left behind. When, later, they reach the summit, they can see the whole way. Here, on earth, we are travellers who have come from other stars or planets. We have no remembrance of them, because we are still too low down, but when we are further up, on other stars, our spiral course will be revealed to us, and when we see it we shall remember the past'.[1]

The souls of our loved ones do not leave us: they watch over, care for and console us. They are media-

[1] Alberto Mario, *Teste e figure* (Padova, 1887, p. 534) states that he had heard these things 'from his own lips, one day in London', and observes that the theory had been appropriated from the writings of Jean Reynaud, a follower of Saint-Simon. See Pezzani, op. cit., pp. 362 et seqq. — Jean Reynaud and Pierre Leroux, who had both left the group of Saint-Simonists headed by Enfantine (Charléty, op. cit., pp. 172 et seqq., 185) soon separated from one another precisely on this question of a future life, Leroux being convinced that the souls of men remain upon earth to experience successive reincarnations in different living beings, while Reynaud upheld the theory of their pilgrimage through the immensity of space. See Weill, op. cit., pp. 158, 160; Thomas, op. cit., p. 58.

tors between us and God. 'All that we call inspiration, force, *virtù*, the urge to sacrifice ourselves, may well be the quickening contact of the soul we love.' Christianity has glimpsed this truth, representing it as the intercession of saints and angels. 'We see in the angels the souls of the righteous, who lived in faith and died in hope; in the guardian angel that inspires us we see the soul that on earth loved us with the most constant and saintly love, and was beloved by us; its reward is the mission and the power to watch over and help us.'

From here it would be but a short step into spiritualism; a step that Mazzini does not take. 'When men no longer believe in God, God in his vengeance makes them believe in Cagliostro. All this farrago about table-turning and spirits babbling alphabetically I know not what foolish answers to what foolish questions, angers me as a profanation of the sanctity of death.' Nevertheless, the possibility of communication with the dead is not to be excluded; but only 'at exceptional moments, with faith and love, when moved by enthusiasm or grief; in the night-time, in solitude, with a supreme effort of concentration and of will'. It seems that he himself believed that he had seen visions of his dead mother.

Thus the theology of the new faith, in other words, 'the conception of God, of life or rather of future lives, and of the law that governs individual destinies, will be more clearly-defined, more pure and more all-embracing than in Christianity'.

8

THE NEW MORALITY

THE new moral system will take to itself all the old, immortal Christian morality; but the latter would be 'imperfect and insufficient to direct and regulate modern life' unless combined and fortified by new principles that correspond with the new stage of human development.

Christianity was an individualist religion. In a corrupt world that was ignorant of the law of progress and of the collective life of humanity, Jesus Christ perceived no other mission for the good of his beloved brethren than that of moral regeneration, and of creating a home in Heaven for them, where all would be free and equal. A necessary condition for their moral improvement was detachment from all earthly things: 'We are weighed down here on earth by sin and temptation.' Christian morality therefore concentrates upon the adoration of God and upon an attitude of resignation towards existing evils as a means of expiation; hence the exclusive importance given to individual purification. Christianity ignores the love of country, 'the love that embraces future generations'. It is 'isolation and refuge, not a warlike mission towards sure and progressive victory'. The political and economic ideas to be inferred from Christian morality extend only to those of equality and freedom; they were summed up in the theory of individual rights.

The new faith, on the other hand, would sanctify the life of this world, as one of the stages leading mankind and individual men towards perfection, and as the means of our purification and approach to the throne of God. Man should not isolate himself 'in sterile contemplation of his own individuality'. 'Each one of us is a part of humanity, we live upon its life and are all called upon to live for it.' 'Men die; but that degree of truth that they have perceived, and the amount of good that they have done, does not perish with them: humanity gathers it up and benefits from it.'

Thus every man must contribute, on earth, towards the attainment of that goal which God has assigned to humanity during each historical period. 'Life is not ours, it belongs to God.' It is not a search for happiness: it is the fulfilment of a duty, 'that of promoting the progress of others, and our own in such a way as to help others'. 'Life is a mission. The fulfilment — more or less continuous and more or less effectual — of this mission constitutes the value and consequently the progress of life.' The individual, therefore, has no rights, or rather, he only has rights in so far as he has duties. 'The sacred formula of Duty must predominate over all. Man's only natural right is to be free from every hindrance to the carrying out of his duty. All the rest are derived from the obligations that we have assumed as a result of our work.'

Here, therefore, is the new moral principle that was to conciliate conflicting interests and to replace the anarchy and dispersion of strength caused by the struggle for individual rights, by agreement upon the attainment of humanity's collective aim. 'It is a matter of finding an educative principle that is superior to the theory of individual rights and that will guide men towards God, teaching them steadfastness in sacrifice and binding them to their brothers without making them dependent on the idea of a single leader or of the strength of all. This principle is Duty.' Duty can have no origin other than that of the Divine Will: 'Without God, where would duty lie? Without God, you will find no basis to any social system other than that of blind, tyrannical, brute force.' 'God, Duty, Social Order: three terms necessarily connected, three concepts which, if one is missing, remain without any meaning.'

The fundamental duty of every man is to seek, with a pure heart and with the fervour born of *intuition* — 'without pride or hypocritical modesty' — that part of Truth that God reveals to man in the historical period in which he lives.

Having found the truth, it is his duty to make it known and to put it into effect. 'We are here on earth to transform, not to contemplate creation. The world is not merely a spectacle; it is a field of battle, upon which those who care for the Good, the Holy and the Beautiful, whether they are soldiers or leaders, victors or martyrs, must play their part.' 'It is not enough for thought to be based upon truth; the life of the thinker must express it, must represent it visibly in his actions; his life must be an unceasing harmony between *mind* and *morality*, between the idea and its application.' '*Thought and Action.*' 'Preach, Fight, Act.'

No man should expect happiness or rewards in this life for his own work. 'Providence sees humanity rather than individual men. It has laid down a general law of progress for the human race; and it has established, furthermore, that all men must help in the development of this law. This is the mission entrusted to each one of us. At the end of our mission, we shall find peace and happiness: sooner or later, according to how much good we have done. But the life, or the intermediate lives, that are given us, have no law of happiness or anything of the sort. The most virtuous man may be profoundly unhappy all his life, but must not for this reason repudiate Providence. Providence assures us of a port; but before reaching it, our passage may be very stormy.' 'Life is a mission. Virtue is sacrifice. Sacrifice alone is holy. Christ has said so, in word and deed. And we must not throw down our cross in the mire because it is heavy. Let us work for the Good, and care for nothing else.' 'The sword shines menacingly before our eyes: affliction awaits us without; and nevertheless our Lord has said: *go forth, go forth, without rest* — But whither shall we go, O Lord? — *Go forth and suffer, ye that are to suffer; go forth and die, ye that are to die.*'

9

THE NEW POLICY

WHAT, then, is the goal that God proposes for mankind in the historical period that will be opened by this new revelation?

The new epoch will be, not that of the individual man, but a *social epoch* in which the thoughts and actions of all those who believe in Humanity will be turned towards Association.

Liberty and equality, which preceding faiths have regarded as ends in themselves, will in the new epoch fulfil their function as a stage in the attainment of Association, according to the method of progressive revelation.

'Association is only the *way of progress*. In this sense a tendency towards Association began with progress that started in the early days of our planet. All the same, if it has always exercised an influence over us, it has done so without our knowledge.' However, when a law is no longer ignored, but proclaimed, recognized and accepted, then 'it is incumbent on us to submit all our actions to it: fulfilment of the law becomes the aim of every endeavour and every thinker examines how best to turn it to advantage. The time has come for the principle of association, solemnly and universally proclaimed, to become a starting-point for the study, both theoretic and practical, of the progressive regulation of human society. It should appear at the head of our constitutions, our legal codes, and our articles of faith'.[1]

Association implies the association of equals, 'since no association is possible except that of free men, and liberty can only exist between equals'. 'Just as liberty can only be established by the conquest of equality, so equality cannot be won save through the Social Epoch, in other words, by the association of all men with a given object in view.' 'Let us believe in Liberty, without which all human responsibility disappears; in Equality, without which Liberty is only an illusion; in Fraternity, without which Liberty and Equality are only a means without an end; and in Association, without which fraternity would be unattainable.' 'Liberty is the basis, and Equality the guarantee, of association. Each new step towards association must be accompanied by further development in liberty and equality.'

The new doctrine, therefore, 'embraces as though within a triangle, the two great principles of liberty and equality, already conquered intellectually by the world, and a third greater still, which the world is still seeking: that of Humanity'.

From the principle of Association Mazzini deduces the whole future order of mankind, religious, political, social and intellectual.

[1] The theory of Association is another of Saint-Simon's: see Charléty, op. cit., pp. 45, 66, 151; Isambert, op. cit., pp. 245-6, 297.

When the peoples have 'a common moral faith, a tacit, solemnly recognized agreement enabling them to understand and trust one another', 'that form of nationalism which is now only too widespread, and which hinders the progress of our intellectual life, cutting it off from the surging universal life of millions of our brothers beyond our frontiers', will disappear; mankind will become a 'great confederation of men of all nations, united in the conquest of those rights which God has granted to all his children, and in the fulfilment of the mission for which alone these rights were conceded'. 'The law of Duty, accepted and upheld, will take the place of that tendency to usurp the rights of others, which until now has governed the relations between one people and another. The ruling principle will no longer be that of *getting the better of others*, but rather of *making things better for all men, by the work of all; progress of each for the good of all.*' There will be 'a *patria* for all men, for all nations: the word *foreigner* will die out from every language; and man will greet man, from whatever land he comes, with the name of brother'. 'Humanity means the association of nations: an alliance of nations for the purpose of fulfilling their mission upon earth in peace and love; the setting up, among free and equal peoples, of a social order permitting them to move about without hindrances, to help one another reciprocally and to benefit each from the work of all, in the progressive development of that line of Thought that God has written in their past, in their national idiom and on their faces.'

'Nations are the individuals of Humanity: they must all work for the conquest of the common goal; each according to its own geographic position, its own particular aptitudes and the means with which nature has provided it.' 'Every Nation has a mission, a special office in the collective work, a special aptitude with which to fulfil it: this is its sign, its baptism, its legitimacy.' 'Humanity is a great army, moving to the conquest of unknown territories, against powerful and cunning enemies. The different peoples form the different divisions of this army. Each has a post confided to it; each has a special operation to accomplish; and victory depends on the precision with which these diverse operations are performed.'

Just as every Nation will be associated in the attainment of humanity's aim, so in each nation the citizens will be united in the attainment of a particular national aim. 'Our future lies in association, in unity of belief and of endeavour; this is what constitutes a Nation. Association of all classes, of every individual, in work that is actively directed towards such a goal; the progressive and harmonious development of every faculty, every intellectual, moral and industrial force in the country in support of the great Law of Humanity: it is this that constitutes National life.'

Capital and labour will be associated in the same hands. We shall no longer see 'the property of the idle rich, gained by the work of others and remaining unproductive or corrupting the spirit, while the true producer is dying of hunger as a slave to his fellowman's pretensions and greed'. 'All must produce: those who do not work have no right to live.' 'The remedy for your ills is the union of capital and labour. When Society no longer recognizes any distinction other than that of producer and consumer, or rather, when every man will be both producer and consumer — when the fruits of labour, instead of being shared among a series of intermediaries, beginning with the capitalist and ending with the retailer, which often raises the price of the article by fifty per cent, are reserved for the worker — then a permanent cause of poverty will disappear from among you. Associated work, the apportionment of the fruits of labour, or rather the profits of the sale of produce between the workers in proportion to the work done and to its value: this is the social order of the future. At one time you were slaves; then serfs; then wage-earners. Before long you will be, if you so wish, free producers and brothers in the association of labour.'

'The workers' associations, free, spontaneous, varied in character and founded upon sacrifice, virtue, love and upon economic principles, must gradually transform the present constitution of labour and replace the wages system by the principle that each man's wealth must be in proportion to his work.' 'He who labours and produces has a right to the fruits of his own work; in this lies the right of private ownership. And if the greater or lesser activity in work is a source of inequality, this material inequality is a proof of moral equality, since it is a result of the principle that every man must be rewarded according to his work: he has what he deserves.' 'The social ideal that prevails today in Europe can be defined as follows: abolition of the proletariat; emancipation of the workers from the tyranny of capital concentrated in too few hands; the sharing of produce, or of the work that results from it, according to the work accomplished; the moral and intellectual education of the workers; voluntary association among the workers to replace, as peacefully and progressively as possible, individual, paid work at the mercy of the capitalists. Such is the sum of all reasonable aspirations today. It is not a question of destroying, abolishing, or transferring the wealth of one class to another by violent means; it is a question of widening the scope of consumption, of increasing production, of awarding a larger share to the producer, of opening up to the worker a way of acquiring property and wealth, and of making it possible for every man of proved morality, ability and good will, to find capital and the means to work in freedom. Such ideas are reasonable and little by little they will triumph. Historically, the time is ripe for their triumph. The emancipation of slaves was followed by that of the serfs; that of the working-classes must follow. Human progress has seen the despotic power of kings overthrown by the patrician class; then the privileges of noble rank destroyed by the *bourgeoisie*, an aristocracy of wealth; and now the property-owning, capitalist *bourgeoisie* awaits the destruction of its privileges by means of the people, the workers; until one day society, founded upon labour, will recognize no privilege save that of the wise, directing intellect, chosen by a people enlightened through education, by the development of its faculties and of its social forces.'

'One day we shall all be workers, that is, we shall live upon the rewards of our work in whatever direction it may be exercised. Existence will represent work accomplished.' 'When Christ's arms, which we now see distended on the cross of martyrdom, come together in an embrace for the whole of humanity, when there are no longer brahmins and pariahs, masters and servants, but men and men only — then with a very different faith and a very different love, we shall adore the great name of God.'

The new family will not be based on egoism, nor will it seek 'the well-being of its members in antagonism towards others or in an indifference that is the denial of common brotherhood'; but, 'playing its part in the education of the world, and regarding itself as the germ or nucleus of the nation, it will give the child — between a kiss from his mother and his father's caress — his first lessons in citizenship'. 'Before God the Father there is neither *man* nor *woman*, only the *human being*. Man and woman are the two notes without which there is no human chord. Give woman equality in your civil and political life.' 'The emancipation of women will establish a great religious truth, fundamental to all the rest: the unity of the human race. It will associate in the search for Truth and Progress forces and faculties that today are sterilized by a state of inferiority which starves the soul.'

Poetry, no longer isolated from society and life, but become 'social poetry', 'will bring with it harmony, life and unity'. 'It will sing the destiny of man and will lighten his travail of spirit, teaching him to lift his thoughts to God, by way of Humanity.' 'It will sing the joys of martyrdom, of immortality for the conquered, of grief that expiates and sufferings that purify, of memories and hopes, and the traditions of a world that is giving birth to another. It will murmur words of holy consolation. It will tell the young of what is great in sacrifice: steadfastness, silence, the sense of being alone but of not despairing; of enduring torments that are misunderstood or unknown, and long years of disappointment, bitterness, injuries, with no complaint. It will teach them a belief in future things and how to labour unceasingly in support of such a belief, though with no hope of living to see it triumph.'[1]

[1] These theories, too, on a social art are Saint-Simonist in origin: see Charléty, op. cit., pp. 51, 52, 469; Weill, op. cit., pp. 6, 83, et seqq.; and Thomas, op. cit., pp. 41 et seqq., 53-4.

10

NATIONAL AND DEMOCRATIC REPUBLICS

IF the law of progress brings us to the constitution of Humanity, and Humanity is the Association of single nations and of free and equal peoples, it follows that 'Humanity will not be truly constituted until all the peoples that form it, having won the free exercise of their sovereignty, are united in a republican federation. Nationhood is sacred.' 'The Pact of Humanity cannot be signed by individuals, but by free and equal peoples with a name, a flag and a consciousness of their own life.' 'Without the recognition of free and spontaneously constituted national states, we shall never have the United States of Europe.'

A nation cannot consist of 'a shifting multitude' with no roots in the soil; nor is it a gathering of 'a certain number of men, it matters little whether thousands or millions, independent of one another and only grouped together by virtue of certain common material interests for the satisfaction of which some form of association is necessary'. This is a materialistic theory to be indignantly rejected. 'A nation is the association of all those men who, by reason of their language, the geographical conditions under which they live, and the part assigned to them by history, form a single unit, recognize the same principles, and make their way under the guidance of the same laws towards the same goal. God has prescribed the affirmation of its nationhood to every people as the part it must play in the work of humanity: this is the mission, the task that each people must perform upon earth in order that the Divine Idea may be realized in the world; this is its right to citizenship, the badge of its personality and of the rank that it occupies among its brothers, the Peoples of the world.' 'The Nation must represent an element of progress in European society, a sum of special faculties and tendencies, a way of thought, a people's aspirations, the germ of a common faith, a tradition distinct from those of other nations and one that constitutes an historical unity between past, present and future generations belonging to the same land.' 'Where men do not recognize a common duty to be accepted with all its consequences, where there is no identity of purpose for everyone, no nation exists, but a fortuitous assemblage of individual elements, a mob that will break up at the first crisis; a concourse of men who have come together by chance and are liable to fall, sooner or later, into anarchy; they are not a people, they have no national life and no future.'

'Our country is the sign of our part in the common work, it is the place where God has put the tools we must use in fulfilling our special task; it is the symbol of a mode of thought, of a particular vocation indicated by traditions of race, affinity of tendencies, by a common speech and topographical characteristics.' 'Every Nation is Humanity's worker; it labours for Humanity, in order to attain a common end for the good of all; if it perverts its mission to selfish ends, it declines and must be subjected, inevitably, to a phase of expiation that will last in proportion to its degree of guilt.' 'Where you find a consciousness of the particular goal, and an ability to reach beyond it to the common goal of Humanity, you have a Nation: without this there is only a fraction of a people, destined, sooner or later, to lose its identity in another.'

It follows that the nation must have a centralized political structure, so that the common duty may be proclaimed and all the country's forces dedicated to promoting it in the great association of Humanity. Some central authority, in fact, must define the nation's aims, dispose of its military forces, maintain law and justice, and promote the welfare of the lower classes. It must also carry out such work as national honour and interest may require, and represent the nation in the field of foreign politics; and it must sum up the work achieved, indicate future progress, and direct the national progress along lines that coincide with the common progress of Humanity. 'Where a mission exists, that is, a common destiny to fulfil, there must be an equal, natural tendency towards unity.' 'Nation is a word that represents unity.'

Federalism, which regards the State as a conglomeration of local independent bodies, without a central source of education, thought and action, is, in the political and administrative field, an extension of the now superseded doctrine of individual rights; it is a selfish, materialistic principle; retrograde, anarchical and opposed to all progress and sense of mission. 'The school of social *duty* must, logically and essentially, favour a single central authority. Life for it is simply an office to perform, a mission. The definition of this mission can only be found in the term *collective* as being superior to all the individual elements of a country: it can only be found in the People, in the Nation. If a collective mission exists, a communion in duty, a solidarity between all the citizens of a State, it cannot be represented except by National Unity.'

In opposing Federalism, Mazzini had chiefly in mind the ideas of those moderate Italian liberals who wanted to solve their national problems by means of a league of princes; and he considered Switzerland a typical federal state, as constituted before the reforms of 1848. It would seem that he never knew much about the democratic republican federalism of Cattaneo and Ferrari, and the few Lombard followers of Romagnosi; nor had he any precise idea of the federal constitution of the United States of America. One of the reasons for Mazzini's hostility towards the insurrection of the Paris Communards in 1871 was the Commune's assertion of its own complete autonomy. 'That programme—France to be no longer an Empire nor a single Republic, but to form a federation of small States, provinces and free cities—is derived from materialistic principles.' The theory of the Communards 'dismembers the Nation into thousands of Communes, and leaves them all unlimited freedom to educate themselves or not, as they think fit'.

These centralized national states could only be republican. A nation is, in fact, the association of all its citizens for the attainment of its own specific national aims: and 'true association can only be between those who are equal in their rights and duties. The first consequence of Association and of Equality for all its members is this: that no family and no individual can assume exclusive authority over the whole, or any part, of the forces and activities of the State. Sovereignty belongs to the Nation alone'. 'A republic is the only logical and legitimate form of government.' 'You must confute by every means in your power the foolish idea that the Republic is, for us, simply a question of political form; you must explain that the Republic is not only the natural expression of our nationhood, of our traditions as a people and the pledge of our rise to future greatness, but a *principle* of Education planted at the summit of the whole edifice; a formula of equality for all, of liberty and therefore of responsibility for all, in place of the absurd notion that puts irresponsibility at the top; a precept that bestows office only on merit and achievement, not upon birth or wealth.' 'By Republic we do not mean a form of government, a name, a system imposed on opponents by the victorious side. We mean a moral principle, a new step forward by the People on the way of education, a political institution destined to produce moral progress; we mean the system that must bring about liberty, equality and association.'

Republics must be democratic. 'The second consequence is this: that no class and no individual can assume administration of the social activities and forces in the State without a direct mandate from the nation'; 'laws made by only a small fraction of the citizens can only, in the very nature of things, reflect the thought, aspirations and desires of that fraction; they do not represent the Country, but a third, a quarter of it, perhaps only a class or a district'. 'The man who does not in some way exercise the right of election, ceases to be a citizen: the pact of association, no longer reflecting his will, will be broken, and every law will be, so far as he is concerned, despotic.' 'We believe in the People as the only ruler, the only sovereign, for every State: in the people one and indivisible, that knows no castes or privileges save those of Genius and Virtue; no proletariat nor aristocracy of land or finance, but only abilities and active forces dedicated, for the good of all, to the administration of what is our common stock, this earth.'

'We are at the start of a great Epoch, the Epoch of the Peoples.' 'God and the People: God at the summit of the social structure; the People, the university of our brothers, at the base.' 'You owe allegiance to none save God in Heaven and the People upon earth.'

II

POPULAR THEOCRACY

MAZZINI'S national, unitary, democratic republic is essentially a religious organization. Its fount of sovereignty, as in Catholic theocracy, is God. 'God alone is supreme.' 'God alone is ruler.' 'Sovereignty resides not in the *I* or the *We*, but in God.' The People is worthy to exercise sovereignty in so far as its will is identified with the divine law. It alone can interpret this law, and it alone is 'God's Prophet'.

With Humanity enlightened by the new faith, inspired by the vision and the acceptance of a common religious ideal, the popular will, with no need for intermediaries, would be the means of transmitting the divine will. Election by universal suffrage is the rite through which the 'good' and 'infallible' People, inspired by God, and always ready to recognize 'virtue crowned by genius', though without 'servile adoration', will entrust the direction of national affairs 'to those superior in wisdom and virtue', 'to intellects illumined by devoted work for their country'. They will do this after sternly questioning themselves, seeking in their own conscience and their own tradition the goal appointed for them by God, and after ascertaining their own beliefs, aspirations and needs. 'We can always know men of high intellect and virtue by their works; and who among us would not follow them? Who would not zealously and faithfully obey the laws that they would lay down, laws inspired by our common need and directed towards our common good?'

We shall thus have the true, holy authority for which the world is longing: freely chosen, recognized by all, and joyfully obeyed. It will not hold its duty to be done 'merely by following in the wake of the civilizing spirit that governs the nation', but will know 'how to take the lead in social thought, raising its banner on high so that all may gather round it'.

It follows that in the new order for mankind the dualism between spiritual and temporal power will have no *raison d'être*: for it is 'an immoral conception and, in the nature of things, has no basis'. This is a curious point in Mazzini's thought, coinciding as it does with the most uncompromising of Catholic doctrine.

'Man is one being: you cannot cut him in two and expect him to agree with you on the principles that are to regulate the social order, when he differs from you on the question of his origin, his destiny and the laws governing his life on earth.' 'Nothing is Caesar's, except in so far as it conforms with the divine law. Caesar, in other words the civil power, is only the mandatary, the executor, when its own efforts and the times allow it, of God's design.' It is impossible to separate 'morals from politics, theory from practice, the ideal from the real, and God from the earth'. 'The separation of Church and State is an arm of defence against the injury caused by a Church that is a Church no longer; it may be invoked as a remedy during a period of transition', but 'those who reduce the problem to the formula *A free Church in a free state* are supporting an abomination, and have no spark of moral faith in their souls'. 'No one sees the only reasonable solution to the problem, a transformation of the Church in such a way that it is brought into harmony with the State and directs it, progressively and without despotic methods, upon the way of righteousness.' 'Religion will be the soul of the new State.' 'Religion and politics are inseparable. Without religion, politics can only lead to anarchy and despotism. Religion is the supreme, educative principle; politics are the application of that principle to the various manifestations of human life. To presume, therefore, to separate the things of this world from those of Heaven, the temporal from the spiritual, is not moral, logical or indeed possible.' 'Power is one: the law of the spirit. Religion is in the seat of government: its interpreters, the temporal authorities, put it into practice.' 'The Moral Law, recognized and accepted, must reign supreme: the temporal power has the task of applying it to the civil and economic spheres of life.'[1]

[1] Another theory that is Saint-Simonist in origin (see Weill, op. cit., p. 5; Charléty, op. cit., pp. 72-3); and one that is in full accord with Catholicism. For this reason Donaver ('*Il sentimento religioso di Giuseppe Mazzini*' in the *Rassegna Nazionale*, LV, 448, 451) is not unjustified in urging Catholics to cite Mazzini's authority in combating the supporters of the lay state. But in all else Mazzini was opposed to Catholicism. Such statements as those of Schack (*Guiseppe Mazzini e l'Unità Italiana*,

We do not know precisely in what manner Mazzini would have organized the two powers and the relations between them. Certainly, the new society would have no priesthood and no papacy. 'Those men who are endowed by God with genius and special virtues, are the apostles of His continual, progressive revelation; the People, the collective sense of Humanity, will interpret it; they will accept the revelation of Truth and transmit it from one generation to another, turning it to practical use, and applying it to the different currents and different activities of human life. Humanity is like a man who lives indefinitely and is always learning. There are not, therefore, nor can there be, men or powers that are infallible: there is not and cannot be a privileged caste that is the depositary and interpreter of the Law; there is not, and cannot be, any necessity for an intermediary between God and man, apart from Humanity.' 'God is God, and Humanity is His prophet.' 'One God: one ruler, God's law; one interpreter of this law, Humanity.' 'The holy Church of the future, the Church of men who are free and equal, will bless all progress made by the Spirit of Truth, will identify itself with the life of mankind, and will have neither pope nor laity, but believers, each one of them a priest with a different office to perform.' It will, in fact, be a

Rome, Soc. Laziale, 1892, p. 57), that Mazzini's religion was 'a Catholicism freed from impurities', of Donaver (*Vita di Giuseppe Mazzini*, Florence, Lemonnier, 1903, p. 235) that 'had the times been different and the Church not opposed to his patriotic principles, Mazzini would not have been averse to accepting Catholicism', and of Giovannini (*Il pensiero economico di Giuseppe Mazzini*, Bologna, Garagnani e figli, 1904, p. 49), that Mazzini, 'like Dante, knew well how to distinguish the evil work of men from the essence of the Catholic doctrine and institution', are all without solid foundation.

religious republic; 'a Constituent Assembly and a Council, these will be the Prince and the Pope of the future'.

The representatives of mankind on the Council will issue a Declaration stating the common aim of all nations; in each national constituent assembly the People will indicate the special aim, and the part of the general work, that concerns its own nation, by means of a national Pact beginning with a Declaration of Principles. 'God and the People for each nation, God and Humanity for all nations.'

It seems, therefore, that the Council of Humanity is destined by Mazzini to function with spiritual authority: it would be formed by 'men venerated for their wisdom, their intellect and their benevolence', elected probably by universal suffrage, and would indicate 'the general mission of the peoples in the sphere of knowledge', 'harmonizing the various enterprises of the different peoples, like the movements of different columns in an army'. Temporal authority would be exercised by the governments of the single nations, according to local needs and requirements, and under the supervision, it would seem, of the Council of Humanity.[1]

We thus have a universal federation of national, republican and democratic states, 'united in brother-

[1] Saint-Simon, too, wanted the government of mankind to be entrusted to a body of wise men and artists elected by the People, who would speak in God's name and study the application of the new law of the universe, which He first indicated in that of universal gravitation and then in that of indefinite progress: 'The strength of the wise men of Europe united in a general corporation bound together by a philosophy based on the idea of universal gravitation would be incalculable.' See Charléty, op. cit., pp. 8-9, 12, 45; Weill, op. cit., p. 5; Isambert, op. cit., pp. 77-8.

hood and in peaceful emulation upon the way of progress'. At the centre of this federation a supreme religious assembly 'will sanctify with its blessing all progress of the spirit, every development of thought and every action made for the benefit of others'. Thus 'human society will be composed, as far as possible, in the image of the divine life: of that heavenly country where all are equal, where all share in the one love and the same happiness'. 'When all the children of God are free, equal and bound together in brotherhood by a common faith expressed in thought and work, and when knowledge of the law is reflected in every life as the sun is reflected in every drop of dew on the flowers of the field, the end will be attained. Humanity, transformed, will then behold another goal before it.'

12

NATIONAL AND DEMOCRATIC REVOLUTIONS

THE duty of believers in the religion of Humanity was to be, first and foremost, that of bringing about the realization of the new way of life.

Before all else, therefore, they were to preach their faith and lead their fellow-men to adopt it. 'The peoples of mankind can only be set free through awareness of the truth. They will not take action until a newly-revealed goal is made known to them, the conquest of which requires the work of all, equality for all and some to take the lead. Without such knowledge there will be no faith, sacrifice or enthusiasm strong enough to be effective.' 'Foundations can only be laid according to moral principles. When you have planted in the nation's heart the principle that the State owes its existence to each one of its members and their work for it, and when you have added the correct definition of existence, you will have prepared a way for the triumph of right over privilege, an end to the exclusive control of one class over another and the end of pauperism. When you have taught men to believe in the other principle, that society is association in work, and thanks to that faith, logically and practically to accept all its consequences, then you will have no more castes or aristocracies, or civil conflicts or crises; you will have a *people*. And when the words: all those who belong to one country are brothers, have made their hearts into a sanctuary for love and virtue, then and only then you will have a Nation.' 'The present problem, the problem that must concern us, is that of education. If we do not attempt, by propagating our faith in certain principles and beliefs, to make men better, to unite them, to turn them from the insensate egoism that devours them, all is useless. Whatever form of government you have, the same inequality and the same wretchedness will recur in a different form.'

The state of two-thirds of Europe, however, was admittedly such as to make any education of this sort impossible. 'Look at Italy. No way lies open there for progress, save that of revolution. Tyranny has raised an impenetrable barrier along her frontiers. A triple army of spies, customs officials and police watches day and night to prevent the circulation of suspect literature. Unorthodox teaching is proscribed. The universities are in a state of slavery, or closed. Capital punishment threatens not only those who print but those who possess or read forbidden books. The introduction of independent or foreign newspapers is prohibited. The intellect dies in childhood for lack of nourishment. Who will give progress to this people? Who will give it to Poland, where similar conditions exist? Who to Germany? How can we introduce the sacred ideals desired by all, into these countries? Insurrection is the only course, so far as I can see, possible for these people; a general, determined rising of the multitude: the holy war of the oppressed.' 'I make a distinction between these countries and ours,' wrote Mazzini in comparing Switzerland with Italy. 'Here there is already freedom of the press, freedom of education, the right of association, etc.; all the means, in fact, for social betterment, without crises and dangerous upheavals. Here progress depends simply on men themselves: therefore education, and the belief in certain principles, is all they need. When I hear men crying out for bloodshed, terror, rebellion, I always disapprove. But with us it is different: there is nothing. Education in nationhood is impossible for us. We must, therefore, first resort to force in order to gain a position in which we can speak, print, teach, develop our faculties, etc., whatever crisis has to be passed through. This is why it is my policy always to repeat: action for us, pacific progress and education for the rest.' As to this revolutionary action necessary for Italy and the other enslaved countries, 'If one attempt fails, the third or fourth will be successful. And if failure is repeated, what matter? The people must be taught not resignation but steadfastness: they must learn how to rise and be defeated and rise again a thousand times, without becoming discouraged.'

Insurrection, to succeed, must be universal. 'We are stronger in every way than our oppressors. When we rise simultaneously throughout all our sphere of action, we shall win. We must oppose the league of princes with a Holy Alliance of the peoples.' 'The day that finds us all united, in agreement upon the work to be done under the watchful eye of the best amongst us, who have fought and suffered most, will be the eve of victory.'

The old powers must be destroyed: 'The Papacy is a lifeless corpse, like the Monarchy.' 'Bury your dead.' 'Neither Pope nor King; only God and the People will open the way of the future to us.' But insurrection is a negative principle; it would remain sterile and without legitimate authority if it were not accompanied by the positive work of reconstruction. It is in this work that revolution consists. 'Insurrection ends when revolution begins. The first is war, the second pacific action. Insurrection and revolution must therefore be ruled by different laws and different standards. Power concentrated in the hands of a few picked men, chosen for their wisdom and resolution by the risen people, must direct the aims of the insurrection and win the battle: but to the People alone belongs the task of directing the revolution.' In other words, 'reforms which in themselves constitute the revolution are the concern of the nation, peacefully represented in a Constituent Assembly'.[1]

The revolution would have to aim at bringing into

[1] From this distinction it would seem that Mazzini makes revolution chronologically distinct from and subsequent to insurrection. But the distinction is more logical than actual, for the words quoted above are followed by the statement that 'the rulers of the insurrection must pass decrees for the immediate amelioration of the poorest classes, so that the people may know that the revolution is beginning for them'.

force the principles proclaimed by the new religious revelation: 'It must translate into practical results every new syllable of God's law'; 'it must be an upward movement of the people on the way of Progress'.

Since in this new phase of history mankind would have a republican form of government and no distinctions or privileges of birth or class would be allowed, it follows that 'the revolution cannot be lasting or legitimate if it does not treat the social problem in conjunction with the political one'. 'A purely political revolution cannot exist for us. Nor can there be a purely social revolution.'

Above all, free and equal national states were to be set up, which, forming a federation among themselves, would constitute the universal association of the human race. 'European revolution today will be made in the name of national independence. It means the transformation of the map of Europe, and an end to all treaties imposed by conquest, craft or the arbitrament of kings. It means a new order, according to the tendencies and vocations of the peoples, and freely agreed by them; the abolition of all reasons for selfish hostility amongst them; a balance between the forces of the different groups, and therefore the possibility of brotherly relations between the peoples.' 'Nationhood: this is the sign, the meaning and the dominating idea of the new Epoch.' 'The realization of national independence is not merely reparation for great injustice; it is the consequence of a historical and philosophical conception, the substitution of feudal monarchies by the principle of popular sovereignty, and the logical application of our faith in freedom; it is also a necessary step towards association and the apportioning of collective work; the constitution of an instrument to enable an immense sum total of moral, intellectual and economic forces, now lost or diverted into the continual struggle against despotism and the misgovernment that results from despotism, to co-operate towards the betterment of the whole human family and the increase of collective wealth.' 'The map of Europe[1] must be remade. The new philosophy will only remain theoretical until this re-ordering of Europe has taken place.'

To ensure that, in setting about such a task, no mistakes were made, the map of Europe would have to be studied 'without prejudices, without foolish ambitions or pride in country, and in a strictly religious spirit', in order to observe 'God's design clearly traced upon it in the great river courses, in the lines of the mountain ranges and in other geographical conditions'. Mazzini, contenting himself with indicating only the 'main lines' of reconstruction, and 'leaving details to the future and the people's vote', foresaw the formation of 'thirteen or fourteen national groups':

1. The Iberian Peninsula, in which, sooner or later, Spain and Portugal would attain political union.

2. France, in which national unity 'is irrevocably laid down'.

[1] For Mazzini 'Humanity' generally means Europe. He does not attach much importance to the United States of America. The world outside Europe would seem to be assigned to the different European nations as spheres of influence where their civilizing mission should be carried out.

3. Great Britain, where 'the fusion of its three races, Scandinavian, Germanic and Celtic, as yet imperfect, is only a matter of slow, internal administrative progress'.

4. The republican confederation of Holland and Belgium.

5. Scandinavia, embracing Norway, Sweden and Denmark.

6. Germany, divided into two large administrative sections: the first consisting of the Archduchy of Austria, Bavaria, Württemberg, Hesse-Darmstadt, etc.; and the second of Prussia, Saxony, Hanover and the other twenty-seven or twenty-eight lesser sovereign states. Alternatively, Germany might be made into a 'tripartite confederation consisting of the zones running parallel with the Oder from Stettin to Ratisbon, with the Elbe from Koenigstein to its mouth, and with the Rhine'.[1]

7. Switzerland, 'changed into an Alpine Confederation, with the addition of Savoy on the one hand and the Austrian Tyrol on the other, and extending to such other territories as are peopled by mountaineers who would seem the natural brothers of the Swiss'.

8. Italy: the most clearly-defined nation in Europe, from the furthest point of Sicily to the line of the Alps.

9. Greece, with the islands of the archipelago, Epirus, Macedonia, Rumelia, and reaching as far as Constantinople, to raise a powerful barrier there against the danger of Russian incursions into Europe.

[1] This passage was written in 1858. In 1861 Mazzini was hoping for complete national unity for Germany. After the war of 1870 he deplored the annexation of Alsace-Lorraine 'without the free consent of its citizens'.

10. Illyria or Southern Slavonia, which would embrace the confederated states of Carinthia, Croatia, Dalmatia, Bosnia, Montenegro, Serbia and Bulgaria.[1] Between 1832 and 1852 Mazzini thought that the lead in this confederation should be taken by Hungary, around which country the Southern Slavs and the Roumanians would gravitate as 'political satellites'; in 1857, although regarding Hungary as a country in which the Magyar element would in time be absorbed by the Slav, he detached it from the Southern Slavs and associated it with Roumania; in 1858 he joined it in a confederation with Bohemia, Moravia and Roumania, in 1871 he said that Hungary, 'uprooted from the Austrian Empire, could be joined to Germany'.

11 and 12. Two confederations, to the north of the preceding one: in 1857 one of these was to consist of Bohemia, Moravia and the Slovak tribes of Hungary, while Hungary, 'reconstituted as a Slavonic power', was to be united to Roumania. In 1858 the two confederations were to be united outright, in a single organization comprising Bohemia, Moravia, Hungary and Roumania. In 1871, Roumania, with Transylvania, was to be autonomous. It would seem that in this part of Europe 'God's design' was less clearly to be discerned than Mazzini liked to believe.

13. Poland, reconstituted within the frontiers of 1772.

14. Russia.

In the work of Humanity, a special mission awaited

[1] Mazzini seemed to have no knowledge of any specifically Albanian problem.

every one of these national organizations: 'And at the head of each shall be emblazoned the sign of a special mission: upon that of Britain, *Industry and Colonies*; of the Poles, *Slavonic leadership*; of the Muscovites, *the civilizing of Asia*, of the Germans, *Thought*, of the French, *Action*; and so forth, from people to people.'[1]

Within this new European order there is no longer any place either for the Austrian Empire or for Turkey. 'The Austrian Empire does not represent a nation; it represents the administration, by force, of a number of peoples divided from one another by language and habits, and intended, from their origins, beliefs, and special aptitudes, to develop in different ways. In Eastern Austria, the Turkish empire in Europe, about fifteen million Europeans — Slavs, Greeks and Roumanians — almost all of them Christian in their beliefs, are subjected to the absolute rule of a million and a half Asiatics, who, encamped upon their land in the name of a radically different religious faith, that of Mahommedanism, have no sort of affinity with them, whether of language, customs, traditions or sympathies . . . The Turkish Empire, like the Austrian, is condemned to perish rapidly; like the Catholic Papacy, the Moslem Papacy will disappear, before the end of the century.'

[1] A theory drawn from the followers of Saint-Simon (see Charléty, op. cit., pp. 44-5, 142-3) who in their turn had borrowed it from the eighteenth-century German pre-romantics.

13

ITALY'S MISSION: THE THIRD ROME

ITALY'S great mission was to be that of taking the lead in setting up the new order for mankind.

Italy, wrote Mazzini in 1844, was oppressed and disunited. 'We have no flag of our own, no name in politics, no voice among the nations of Europe: we have no common centre, no common agreement, no common market. We are broken up into eight states that are independent of one another, without a united aim, without alliances and without regular reciprocal contact. Eight customs barriers – not counting the internal ones for which the corrupt administration of each state is responsible – obstruct our material progress and interests, and prevent the development of our industries or any widespread commercial activity. Embargoes or heavy tariffs strike at our imports. Agricultural or industrial products lacking in one province of Italy, abound in another, yet no possibility exists of selling or exchanging what is superfluous. Eight different systems of currency, of weights and measures, of civil, commercial and penal legislation and of administrative restrictions keep us as strangers one from another. And all these states that divide us are despotically governed, without participation of any sort by the people. One of these states, containing almost a quarter of the population of Italy, belongs to a foreign power, Austria. The others, either owing to family bonds or to their own weakness, never oppose Austria's will.'

However, an Italian nation indubitably exists and is destined to form a great national state. 'There are not five Italies, or four Italies, or three Italies. There is only one Italy. God who, in creating her, smiled upon her land, has awarded her the two most sublime frontiers in Europe, symbols of eternal strength and eternal motion, the Alps and the sea. Let whomsoever should presume to assign her others be thrice accursed by you and those who come after you. From the immense circle of the Alps, resembling the vertebral column that constitutes the unity of the human frame, a marvellous chain of unbroken ranges descends to the sea, and beyond it, in Sicily. Wherever Italy is not encircled by the Alps she is enclosed, as in a loving embrace, by the sea: that sea which our forefathers called *Mare nostro*. And dispersed about the sea, like gems fallen from her diadem, lie Corsica, Sardinia, Sicily and other smaller islands, where the nature of the soil, the lie of the land, the language and the spirit of the people, all speak of Italy. Within these confines other races have come, one after another, to conquer and oppress: but they have never been able to erase the sacred name of Italy, nor to extinguish the innate energy of the race that first peopled her. The Italic element, more potent than any other, has worn down the religion, language and customs of her conquerors, and has superimposed upon them the stamp of Italian life.' 'You are twenty-five million men, endowed with splendid faculties: you have a glorious tradition that is the envy of other nations. Before you lies a great future. Let not a single one of those twenty-five millions be excluded from your pact of brotherhood; let not a single glance but that of a free man be raised to the heavens above you. Rome shall be the holy Ark of your redemption: the temple of your nation.'

'National unity was and is the destiny of Italy.'

If, then, Italy is to achieve unity, she must destroy two obstacles: the Papacy and Austria. Rome is not only the 'true capital of Italy', without which national unity is impossible; she is 'the seat of the Papacy: of that Institution which is the source of all arbitrary power in Europe; which holds the human soul in bondage, and prohibits any future religious development, divorcing it from the progress of humanity, indeed, setting religion in opposition to progress. Freedom for Rome means freedom for the world. Rome cannot rise again without proclaiming the triumph of God over idolatry, of eternal truth over falsehood, and the inviolability of humanity's conscience'. 'The Papacy will remain until the new-born Italy dislodges it from the throne where it slumbers. The crux, then, of the whole European question lies in Italy. To Italy belongs the high office of solemnly proclaiming European emancipation. And Italy will fulfil the task with which she has been entrusted.' 'Europe wanders in the void, seeking new bonds that will unite within one religion all the beliefs, expectations and vital forces of those individuals who, isolated now by doubt, are without a heaven and consequently without the power of transforming the earth. And this longed-for unity, O Italy, can only come from your country and from you: it can only be emblazoned upon the banner that will be raised high above the two landmarks — the Campidoglio and the Vatican — that record the course of thirty and more centuries of humanity's life.' 'From Rome alone can the word of modern unity go forth, because from Rome alone can issue the absolute destruction of the old unity.' In a regenerated Rome a universal Council of wise men will meet to lay down the dogma of the new faith. The Italian people are to be the Messianic people, who will initiate a new epoch of the human race.

The struggle, too, against Austria to which Italy is inevitably called will have consequences universal in their implications. 'Look at the central and eastern parts of Europe. There you can see, spread out and intertwined with one another like a nest of serpents, owing to the similarity of the races caught up in the coils, two great empires upon which rests the whole structure of European despotism and the negation of the principle of nationhood: the Austrian Empire, symbol of immobility, a veritable European China; and the Turkish Empire, symbol of Asiatic fatalism, an Oriental Papacy always in opposition to European progress.' 'The destinies of these two empires are intimately connected. Life cannot enter into one without causing some stir in the other.' 'The enemy with which Italy has to contend is holding down peoples who long for liberty; and beyond the frontiers of Austria, in the lands subject to the tyranny of the Turks, there are signs of revolt among many peoples, in origin identical with those under Austrian rule. For this reason, every blow we deliver against the Austrian Empire will break a link in the chain that extends from the valley of the Danube to Eastern Europe.'

In assailing Austria, therefore, Italy would promote the setting up of independent states among all these oppressed nationalities, and would thus provide the elements of a future European United States; while at the same time, by destroying Papal rule in Rome, she would clear a way for the new faith that was to bind the future confederation of Humanity together. 'Italy cannot live, unless she lives for all. We can only live a European life, and can only free ourselves by freeing others. We must be great or perish. Rome and Venice are today the emblems of our mission. We cannot have Rome without giving Europe a new faith, and without freeing Humanity from the incubus of the past: we cannot have Venice without destroying the double symbol of despotism in Central and Eastern Europe, and initiating the era of national independence.' 'What for others may be simply a moral duty, is a law of life for us.' Mankind must be raised up by Italy upon the ruins of the Papacy, the Nation upon those of the

Empire. 'The destiny of Italy is that of the world.'

It is with filial pride that Mazzini adduces the past glories of Italy in confirmation of his prophecies. Had not Italy always been a civilizing influence among the nations, a pioneer of social and religious unity in Europe? Was not the Italic genius essentially of a religious bent? And had not Italy been the only country to send forth, not once but twice, a call to unity among the nations? 'Come with me. Follow me to the wide *campagna* that, thirteen centuries ago, was a meeting-place for every race, and I will show you where the heart of Italy beats. Here Goths, Ostrogoths, Erulians, Lombards and many others, barbarians or semi-barbaric, came down, without knowing it, to receive the blessing of Italic civilization, before setting forth again for other lands; and the dust that the wayfarer shakes from his feet is the dust of many peoples. All is now changed and there is a silence in the wide and lonely spaces that fills the soul with the sadness evoked by a graveyard. But he that, strong in faith and purified by suffering, pauses at nightfall in this solitude, when the sun's last ray has died upon the great sweep of the horizon, will become aware that beneath his feet there is a murmur as of awakening life, the quickening of generations yet to come, who await the *fiat* of a life-giving word before coming to repopulate these wastes, which seem made for a Council of the Peoples. And I understood this ferment, and cast myself upon the ground in adoration, for it seemed to me a sound full of augury for the future. Stop and look about you, as far as the eye can reach . . . Yonder, like a lighthouse in the immensity of the ocean, there rises a sign of distant greatness. Bend your knee and worship: there beats the heart of Italy; there, in eternal dignity, stands Rome. That salient point upon the horizon is the Capitol of the Christian world. And a few steps from it stands the Capitol of the pagan world. Those two adjacent worlds await a third, greater and more sublime than they, which will rise from among their ruins. This is the Holy Trinity of History, and its Word is in Rome. Tyrants and false prophets may delay the incarnation of the Word, but none can prevent its coming. Although many cities have perished, and all in turn may pass away from this earth, Rome, by the design of Providence, and as the People have divined, is the *Eternal City*, to which is entrusted the mission of disseminating the Word that will unite the world. Her life will be reproduced on an ever widening scale. And just as, to the *Rome of the Caesars*, which through Action united a great part of Europe, there succeeded the *Rome of the Popes*, which united Europe and America in the realm of the spirit, so the *Rome of the People* will succeed them both, to unite, in a faith that will make Thought and Action one, Europe, America and every part of the terrestrial globe. And one day, when the Pact of the New Faith shines forth upon the gathered peoples from the Pantheon of Humanity, which will be raised between the Capitol and the Vatican, dominating both, the age-long dissension between earth and heaven, body and soul, matter and spirit, reason and faith, will disappear in the harmony of life. These things will come to pass when you understand at last that the Life of a people is religion: when, consulting solely tradition and your own conscience, you become the priests not of righteousness alone, but of Duty, and uncompromisingly wage war not only upon the civil power of Falsehood but on Falsehood itself, which today usurps the name of Authority in Rome; and when you take up again the prophetic cry that Rome, re-awakened, sent out ten years ago [in 1849] to all Italy, and write upon your hearts and on your banner: *We acknowledge one God in Heaven, and one interpreter of His law upon earth, the People.*'

14

ASPECTS OF MAZZINI'S DOCTRINE

SUCH are the religious, political and social theories of Giuseppe Mazzini. Among them are many democratic ideas that belong to our own time, embodied in a Utopian theocratic system resembling those in which medieval scholasticism was so prolific: a fusion of Dante's *De Monarchia* with Rousseau's *Contrat Social* and the doctrines of Saint-Simon, achieved by a nineteenth-century Italian patriot and revolutionary.

It is easy to find weaknesses in such a structure, raised as it is by methods so foreign to our own modes of thought; or to point out the many contradictory statements with which it abounds, and its dubious historical foundations.

To take the law of progress alone — the corner-stone of the whole system — it would be necessary, before accepting the forecast of the future that Mazzini bases upon it, to agree that his statements regarding the different historical periods and their religious character were accurate: which no historian would be prepared to do. We should then have to admit that the succession of events — given that they did in fact occur according to the Mazzinian scheme — represented progress: only to find ourselves faced by the probably insuperable difficulty of defining in what, objectively speaking, progress consists. Finally, even admitting that history has evolved as Mazzini would have us believe, and that its development has represented continual progress, so that we may legitimately maintain, on the evidence of all past centuries, that such progress does exist, it would still remain to be proved that mankind, in the future, might not choose other ways and means of achieving it than those laid down by Mazzini; or even that they might not cease to progress at all.

If, however, from this basic assumption of Mazzini's we turn to examine some of his other assertions, doubts and objections rise at every step. We are entitled to question, for instance, whether universal suffrage has ever been the means through which the will of God has revealed itself to man. Universal suffrage is merely the method by which the party in power can be changed without violence when it has lost the confidence of the majority in the electorate. The revolutionary multitudes inspired by God which Mazzini saw ready to rise on every side were but figments of his own imagination. Mazzini did not know Italy. He had been born into a well-to-do family of Genoa, and had travelled no further than Tuscany, which he visited for a few days, before going into exile. He never made any direct acquaintance with the lower classes in different parts of the peninsula, where the 'people' were indifferent to politics and, indeed, altogether reactionary. In Austria, Germany, Russia and Turkey they were even more inert than in Italy. In Mazzini's time national sentiment prevailed only among the Italian middle-classes.

Traditional religious creeds have never merged into any new revelation. And Mazzini's system, founded as it was on the assumed existence of a revolutionary 'people' inspired by God was at fault on other points. Mazzini saw in Europe nations divided from one another by so-called 'natural' frontiers, traced by God from all eternity in the rivers, mountains and seas. In reality, it is only in exceptional cases that a nation occupies territory endowed with obvious geographical frontiers. England's frontier is the sea. The frontiers of Spain and Italy are the sea and the mountains. For almost all the rest, natural frontiers do not exist. France has natural frontiers on all sides except towards the East, where, in the Rhineland, French and Germans are divided by no well-defined natural boundary. There is no natural frontier between the Germans and the Poles, between the Poles and the Russians, or between the territory occupied by the Roumanians and that of the Magyars. Indeed, Roumania is split up into two parts by a clear-cut natural boundary, that of the Carpathian Mountains. No natural frontier divides Canada from the U.S.A., or the U.S.A. from Mexico. Even the British nation is no longer confined within its own natural frontiers, for during the last centuries it has sent its people out to settle in all parts of the world.

The doctrine of 'natural frontiers' springs from a

scholastic equivocation. The geographers, for the purpose of their studies, classify the surface of the earth into 'natural regions'; though even these vary according to different schools of thought. But in actual fact, human groups, in taking possession of the land, have never concerned themselves with such classifications. National frontiers are a product of human will through history. They are the result of struggles between neighbouring groups, each seeking to expand at the other's expense. 'National' frontiers are historical and artificial. They are the work of man.

And why, one may well ask, should Mazzini associate Denmark, Norway and Sweden in a single unit, and divide Germany into two? Or offer her, as he does in 1858, the right to opt for a tripartite Confederation, and, in 1861, for total unification? And why should Switzerland be afflicted with a confederation, when the law of progress implies political unification for all nations? And how is it that — for all his talk of Humanity — the peoples of the world, outside Europe, are wholly absent from Mazzini's thoughts?

Mazzini overlooked the fact that very few national groups form compact units in themselves. Many of them radiate out from their central nuclei, with the result that there are territories in which offshoots from different nationalities are intermingled. Even the Italian people are not alone in inhabiting the territory south of the Alps: there are Germans in the South Tyrol, and, in Istria, Slavs intermingled with Italians. In Mazzini's time, in most countries, the less civilized national minorities were crushed beneath the civil, military and ecclesiastical bureaucracies, mainly drawn from the predominant nationalities. The subject peoples had not yet reached a clear and active consciousness of their individuality: they were 'nations without history'. But after Mazzini's death, every national group gained a sense of its own identity. His doctrine entitled them to self-determination. Thus, in mixed territories, minorities feel entitled to claim their personal, national and political rights against the privileges of the ruling race. According to Liberal doctrine — if one is to be consistently Liberal — no national group is entitled to stifle the national consciousness of individuals belonging to another nationality in mixed territories, or to violate the personal and political rights of their fellow-citizens. Some kind of compromise must therefore be found in order to grant equal rights to all. Liberal doctrine upholds the rights not only of majorities against the privileges of a minority, but asserts a yet higher justice: the safeguarding of the rights of minorities threatened with the oppression of sectarian majorities. The problem of racial minorities is merely part of a general problem: that of the legal status of all minorities, whether religious, political, social or national. And the problem cannot be solved unless the idea of compulsory unity is abandoned, and the criterion of freedom for all loyally accepted. But most men are led by self-interest and their own passions, rather than by doctrines aimed at establishing justice and peace. As a rule, national majorities in mixed territories claim the right of self-determination for themselves against foreign domination, but deny personal and political rights to their own minorities. And the minorities do the same. The result is that in all mixed territories bitter struggles are carried on in support of 'historical rights' on the one hand, and 'national rights' on the other. This is one of the most dangerous sources of moral and political disorder today.

Mazzini, in his ignorance of the problem, maintained that each nation must keep itself immune from foreign infiltration on the territory assigned to it. This would imply the violent expulsion, extermination or assimilation of all alien groups by the ruling race. Such brutality would be wholly opposed to the humane spirit with which all Mazzini's thought is imbued. But his system would logically lead to it.

Another weak strand in his doctrine concerned international relations. Mazzini gave a purely moral form to what he termed the Association of Humanity. He was preaching national independence to all peoples at a time when many of them were wholly lacking in political consciousness. For this reason he stressed, first and foremost, the necessity of breaking every bond that subordinated nation to nation. He refused to accept any form of legal restriction on the independence of each national unit. He would uphold today the doctrine of unlimited national sovereignty. At the same time he wanted national sovereign states to live in peace under the rule of justice; oblivious of the fact that this would entail putting limits upon national sovereignty and was an inherent contradiction. Mazzini solved the problem by asserting that the peoples, once they were free and equal, would be inspired by God with the spirit of justice; and that therefore there would be no need of any compulsion to keep the peace between them. His Association of Mankind was to be simply a system of moral obligation, freely proclaimed by the best among each people, and freely accepted by the conscience of all.

This was not solving the problem: it was evading the issue by means of an entirely unwarranted assumption. In reality, the peoples of this earth are not divinely inspired with an unmixed sense of justice. They are influenced also by other passions, such as blind egoism, the urge to oppress the weak, and revenge. To make Mazzini's doctrine work, the impossibility of reconciling unlimited national sovereignty with international peace and justice would have to be recognized. But even so, the problem of how to subordinate men's interests, habits, passions and prejudices to such a system would remain.

15

THE PROBLEM OF LIBERTY

ALL the problems raised by Mazzini's teaching lead, sooner or later, to a single problem: what is the place of liberty in this doctrine?

Mazzini never asserts that unanimity for mankind is either possible or desirable: indeed, he considers minority heresies as a 'pledge of future progress', and declares that in the new order of Humanity freedom of thought and freedom for heretical belief will be scrupulously respected, because 'thought must only be confuted or destroyed by thought'. It seems that he wants the 'free and educated individual man' to be 'a prophet of future progress'; a function that will consist in 'protesting, in the name of a new goal beyond the immediate one, against any tendency towards the negation of indefinite progress, and against intolerance'. But the individual, though free to think as he likes and to preach his own heresy, must obey the will of the majority, as legally made known; because 'when the people, the collective body of your brothers, declares that such is its belief, you must bow your head and refrain from any act of rebellion'. 'He who withdraws himself, even for a moment, in his actions, from the general line of thought and the national aim, is acting apart from the vital conditions of Association; and this must not be.'

How, then, can the obligation to obey the people, the interpreter of the divine revelation, be reconciled with the right of free belief in heresy as the herald of new progress? Would not the People, too — imbued, according to Mazzini, with the spirit of the God he has wrested from the Catholic Church and from the monarchies, with their claims to Divine Right — become for this very reason, like the Popes and Kings, an infallible idol with whom none would be permitted to disagree?

Mazzini's theory of liberty in general and of the political liberties in particular, is a 'Jacobin' theory that, with its deified People, might well lead to a totalitarian Theocracy more oppressive than any lay dictatorship.

Freedom, for Mazzini, is not the right of all men to use their own faculties in whatever direction they like, without injury to others: 'True freedom does not consist in the right to choose evil, but in the right to choose from among the different ways that lead to good.' 'Freedom is a means for good, not an end.'[1] Freedom, therefore, is to be known by the choice of means, not the end, which will be indicated by the people's interpretation of the Divine will. These are dangerous maxims, which might well lead to the abolition of all liberty.

But Mazzini, in one of his not rare contradictory

[1] A Catholic and Saint-Simonist theory: Charléty, op. cit., pp. 107-8.

statements, also affirms that freedom of choice between good and evil must be respected, because 'without liberty, morality could not exist, since, if there were no freedom of choice between good and evil, between devotion to common progress and the spirit of selfishness, there would be no responsibility'. He declares that it is the individual's duty to vindicate his freedom even against the people's will 'in the essential things of life'. And he constructs around the different aspects of political freedom — personal freedom, freedom of movement, of religious belief, of opinion, of expression in print or by any other pacific means, freedom of association and freedom to trade — a theory that is undeniably liberal.

Yet in vindicating his own freedom against possible transgression by the majority in the case of 'the essential things of life', the individual only has a 'right of protest in such ways as circumstances may suggest': a statement that is, in truth, altogether too elastic, and that does not succeed in masking some uncertainty in the thought. And from the number of freedoms that are to be respected — here the logical consequences of his system may be perceived — freedom of education and academic freedom are explicitly excluded: since it is through education that the younger generation learns what is good and what is bad, and the moral goal for which the individual must strive in co-ordinating his efforts with those of the nation and of humanity. 'This cry of academic freedom arose (and it is still of value) wherever moral education is the monopoly of a despotic government, of a reactionary caste, or of a priesthood naturally hostile towards the dogma of progress. It has been a weapon against tyranny; a watchword of emancipation, imperfect but indispensable. Make use of it wherever you find yourselves treated as slaves. But I speak to you of a time in which religious faith will have written the word Progress upon the doors of the temple, and all institutions will, in a different form, repeat that word'. Then the nature of the problem will be changed: it will be the State's task to lay down regulations that will 'make a national Education universal, compulsory and uniform in its general direction, for without unity of education there is no nation'.[1] One of the faults with which Mazzini charged monarchical institutions was that of appointing 'a professor of materialist views in one university, a Catholic in another, and a follower of Hegel in a third'; and in writing to Daniel Stern, with reference to the Hegelians who were teaching at Naples and the possibility of an imminent republican revolution, he added: 'In due time we shall sweep all that stuff away.'

In the last years of his life this subject became one of his *idées fixes*. On November 26th, 1870, he wrote to Aurelio Saffi: 'Having to prove how the Monarchy is lacking in all branches of moral judgment, I need a work on the Universities and on university studies in

[1] Saint-Simon, too, wanted a *national catechism*, on social, moral and scientific lines: 'public instruction shall be made uniform everywhere, and the ministers of the different sects must neither preach nor teach anything in conflict with the national catechism'. (Isambert, op. cit., pp. 87-8, and Charléty, op. cit., p. 68.)

general, with observations on the professors, of which a list would be needed with the beliefs that they profess: a Catholic beside Moleschott, a Rosminian beside Vera, etc.' And on January 12th, 1871, he wrote: 'I am anxious to carry out my work on present conditions in the teaching profession and the effect upon it of atheism in the government: the professors teach materialist, Catholic, Hegelian or any other school of ideas.' On November 8th, 1871, he wrote: 'Try to help me in collecting material on the moral situation in the teaching profession today; university professors preaching opposing doctrines, and so on. I want to write on national education, and naturally I have to expose the contrast between what is, and what ought to be.'[1]

In the same way Mazzini's standard of literary criticism can be explained. Once it is accepted that art and literature must have a social and educative function, it is natural that Mazzini, although endowed by nature with good taste and a most sensitive feeling for art, and capable — when not hindered by his own theories — of admirably acute critical judgment, should measure the value of a work of art simply by its degree of conformity with his own social, political and religious ideals; entirely neglecting its aesthetic form. In Dante he only sees and praises the religious and political ideas, in which he perceives 'the same thought that today is deeply-rooted in our epoch'. He dislikes Petrarch, whose work 'already contained signs of a pagan devia-

[1] R. Foà and A. Casati, *Mazzini e gli hegeliani di Napoli,* in the *Critica* of Benedetto Croce, X, 73.

tion'; and, probably ignorant of his *Sine titulo*, could not appreciate the poet's great work of anti-scholasticism. He had little admiration for Shakespeare, 'who knew nothing of the laws of humanity: the future has no voice in his pages; there is no enthusiasm for great principles'. On the other hand, he had a lively sympathy for Byron, because he saw in him the effects of the desperation to which individualism leads, and 'because in its melancholy and its enthusiasms his work is moral, social and prophetic'. Mazzini was always reluctant, above all in the last years of his life, to recognize the true greatness of Goethe, because Goethe 'found no place in his works or in his sympathies for humanity', his system being 'wholly one of poetic materialism, opposed to the culture of the ideal'. Schiller he exalted, because 'he had sanity of spirit, faith in God and hope in the destinies of mankind, even when he saw it brought low'; his writings 'are an inspiration to sacrifice and noble deeds'. For Foscolo, with his patriotism and misfortunes, Mazzini had a filial devotion. He preferred the Polish religious and patriotic poets to Lamartine and Victor Hugo; showed only contempt for the irreligious Leopardi; and had little sympathy with Manzoni's attitude of resignation. In short, it is clear that since art must have an educative function and freedom of education is suppressed, artistic freedom, too, must be sacrificed on the altar of associated humanity.

It is little wonder, therefore, that the official philosopher of the Fascist dictatorship, Giovanni Gentile, hailed Mazzini as a fore-runner of Mussolini: to produce which metamorphosis he had only to suppress from Mazzini's teaching the rights that freedom bestows, and to leave untouched the duties of discipline. The exaltation of past national glories, and the promise of glory to come, may be an excellent tonic for reviving the self-respect of a people humiliated by foreign domination or internal disruption. But it is also one that may cause a restless and aggressive foreign policy, a lust for conquest — and, consequently, disillusionment, bitterness and unmerited self-contempt — when a country is ruled by men with no sense of balance, unable to distinguish what is possible from what is impossible. Take away the atmosphere of justice and goodness that colours all Mazzini's thought, and one finds that, just as his ideas of liberty can be brought, if somewhat mutilated, into line with Gentile's, so from the Third Rome of Mazzini it is easy to slip — with some necessary falsification — into the Third Rome of Mussolini: with results that the Italians now know to their cost, although unfortunately the disastrous experience has not, as yet, cured them all from the disease of megalomania, or from their weakness for rhetorical excess.

16

MAZZINI'S RELIGIOUS ATTITUDE

GENERALLY speaking, the greater part of Mazzini's assertions are arbitrary and impossible to prove; while those that, individually, correspond with real historical facts and tendencies are deduced from dubious principles, form an integral part of a questionable system, and interpret real facts in such a way as to make them, too, appear suspect; they may be true, but not for the reasons adduced by Mazzini.

'He had little aptitude', as Masci rightly observes, 'for scientific thought, for relentless reasoning or the analysis of facts; and his mistaken ideas on the scientific method were made worse by his mistaken application of them.'[1] With his passionate nature, he was unable to subject himself to the effort of logical clarification and organization which the scientific and philosophic method demands; but he was ready to interpose with supreme self-confidence in the discussion of any system of ideas. He qualified every theory with postulates that were not susceptible of, indeed were foreign to, any sort of critical analysis, and he made himself the begin-

[1] '*Il pensiero filosofico di G. Mazzini*', in the *Rivista d'Italia*, June 1905, p. 114.

ning and end of all rational activity; all of which lessened the force of his attacks on certain moral and political ideals as being materialistic and sterile intellectualism.

In proof of the degree in which Mazzini's reasoning faculty was subordinated to feeling, it is enough to observe him in a moment of crisis: when assailed, in the second half of 1836, by that access of despair and doubt which he has described so vividly. 'When I felt myself alone in the world, except for my poor mother, far away and in distress on my account, I drew back in terror at the abyss before me. Then, in that desert, I was faced by Doubt. Perhaps I was wrong and the world was right. Perhaps the idea that I was following was only a dream . . . That day, when my soul was seared by these misgivings, I felt not only inexpressibly wretched, but like a condemned man conscious of guilt and incapable of expiation . . . How many mothers had already wept because of me! How many more would weep if I were to persist in my attempt to rouse the youth of Italy to action in the struggle for a united nation? And suppose this nation were only an illusion? What right had I to decide upon the future and to cause hundreds, nay, thousands of men to sacrifice themselves and all that they held most dear? . . . My anguish was such that I felt near to madness. Had my state of mind endured I should have lost my reason and taken my own life.' Did Mazzini, in such terrible suffering of mind, think of overcoming doubt with the weapons of reason? No; he turned for help to a woman, Eleanora

Ruffini; one of those mothers to whom he had already given most cause to weep. 'Women are my advocates with God. While men, for the most part, cry out against us, desert us or slander us, the women I have known have been my most constant and loving friends.' He writes to Eleanora: 'I know not what I would not give for an hour's talk with you, to tell you all that is in my heart and to ask comfort of you, as a holy blessing . . . I would like to speak to you generally of my ideas, and to hear from you — symbol as you are of constancy and resignation — that they are not illusions: *that the mind has not misled the heart, but that the heart has prompted and willed them.* Since the publication of my ideas on faith, humanity, and the future, is a cause of trouble and persecution for me and for your dear ones, do you love me less? Am I an egoist? Do I heartlessly betray my duties as a man? Do I fail in my love for you and my own family? If I were to die a martyr to our faith, to the faith of Jacopo, would I be unfeeling, would I commit a crime? Say nothing of this to anyone else; but if you can conscientiously give me a word of comfort, do so; if not, be silent, I beg you. I shall know that I am wrong. I shall know that I am pursuing a phantom, that my religion is all false belief and must be given up; and I will give it up, because I believe in you as in an oracle, as in the most virtuous, religious soul, purified and perfected by sorrow, that exists on earth.' This is a method no true philosopher would choose in building up and consolidating his system of ideas.

And how were his doubts resolved? After reasoning

things out, according to all the rules of inductive and deductive logic? Alas, no! 'One day I awoke with a tranquil mind, my intellect clear once more, like one who knows himself saved from great peril. The moment of waking had long been one of deep sadness for me, as the consciousness of having to face my troubles returned; and during those months all the unbearable difficulties with which I would have to contend during the day seemed comprised in this instant. But that morning, nature seemed to smile upon me and the light, like a blessing, to refresh the life in my weary veins. And the first thought that flashed upon my mind was this: that I had been misled by my own egoism, and that I had not rightly understood life. As soon as I could do so, I calmly examined everything, and myself, afresh; and I re-made the whole of my moral philosophy . . . I passed from the idea of God to that of Progress; from that of Progress to a new conception of Life, to faith in a mission, and the logical consequence of Duty as the supreme principle. Having reached that point, I swore to myself that nothing in the world should again make me doubt or forsake it.' God, Progress, Mission, Duty: all these appear only when the crisis has been overcome, when serenity and faith have returned, when Mazzini is able to examine himself in peace; in other words, when, having recovered faith in the legitimacy of his own aspirations, he is in possession of the support he needs in constructing — 'with luminous clarity' — his own system, and holds at last the criterion of certainty in his hands. All this happens unexpectedly, after a night of placid sleep, when some beneficent process of recovery has brought refreshment to 'the life in his weary veins'.

Mazzini was above all a man of action. Thought was only of value to him in so far as it could be translated into action, and one form of action in particular. His ideas were not the fruit of an effort to understand things objectively; they were an instrument that served him in modifying things in accordance with the ideal in which his own moral sentiments found satisfaction. He took from the philosophic, political and historical ideas current in his time those elements best suited to his own temperamental needs, and put them in such order as practical necessity required. In so doing, he imagined himself to be a philospher; but even this was largely due to the atmosphere in which his intellectual development had taken place, in a period when it was the fashion to construct philosophical systems that explained the universe. His own attempt, however, was weak and incomplete.

Yet, given Mazzini's particular moral temperament, this very incompleteness and weakness as a thinker is an essential element in the completeness and strength of the man of action. Confronted by Mazzini's definition of God: 'Creator of all that exists; living, absolute thought, of which our world is a ray and the universe an embodiment', Gentile asks: 'Ray or embodiment? Emanative or pantheistic?' and, seeking to understand what Mazzini could possibly have meant by the statement that 'God and the Law are identical terms, and

Humanity is the living Word of God', concluded that Mazzini's ideas were indeterminate, fluctuating and fantastic, and that as a philosopher he was really of little account.[1] This is true enough. But what, after all, is more indeterminate, for those who have a different religious faith, or who are not endowed with that special state of mind in which religion has its roots, than — for example — the Lord's Prayer that a Christian repeats? Who is this Father of ours who is in Heaven? What is his Kingdom? And what the trespasses that we forgive? Nevertheless, not one of us who has learnt this prayer in childhood can think of it without feeling a fervent desire for righteousness, for love, for peace, or without the conviction that its Author, though not a philosopher, was a very wonderful character. It is a prayer that does not present a sequence of ideas, but raises a host of feelings. And it is the same with every religious faith; a more or less logical structure of reasoning arises over a sentimental foundation, and always aspires to the status of philosophy: against which critics of different faiths and of no faith at all aim their shafts. But to the believer, the entirety of these vague, indistinct and undemonstrable sentiments, clothed in a majestic familiar language unchanged by time, remains untouched. In the conception that Mazzini had of God, oscillating always between pantheism and theism, it was precisely this oscillation (as Crespi pointed out) that kept his energy up to a high and constant level; because the apostle-hero could always, and at the same

[1] G. Gentile, in a long review of the book by Bolton King (*Critica*, 1903, p. 459).

time, draw strength and inspiration from two different conceptions of divinity: from the personal God, Who is Father and Law-giver, demanding duty, conflict and sacrifice from him; and from the God in Whom all creation lives, moves and has its being, present always in the spirit of the individual who obeys, fights and suffers, and giving him the faith and strength he needs for his long and desperate ordeal.

We need not, then, stop to criticize the thinker in Mazzini, thereby making the same mistake that he himself made in regarding himself as a philosopher. Let us rather consider the believer, the apostle, the man of action. In other words, having ascertained the content of his religious faith, let us ask what influence it had. How did it direct his actions and those of his followers? And what practical function did it fulfil in the sphere of history?

PART TWO

THE MAN OF ACTION

I

DIRECT AND INDIRECT INFLUENCE OF MAZZINI'S TEACHING

IT is not easy to determine with any accuracy how great an influence such a man as Mazzini has had over his contemporaries, or may continue to have, through his writings and the work of his followers, after his death.

The fact, for example, that some of Mazzini's ideas have been realized or are in process of realization, is not necessarily due, wholly or even in part, to the results of his preaching. It may be that he merely foresaw the course that events would take, and perhaps was not alone in doing so. In this case, his discernment may be admired, but should not be taken for positive, creative action.

In the same way, if some or even many of Mazzini's ideas have been upheld by others more or less near to him in time or place or in their spiritual affinities, this might simply be explained as a coincidence. Mazzini's influence, in such instances, can only be proved when it is explicitly recognized by those subjected to it, or when other positive, if indirect, proofs exist.

On the other hand, certain historical events may have

been brought about by men who have acted under a more or less genuine Mazzinian impulse of which we know nothing. And even when we have knowledge or proof of such an impulse it is not easy to determine how much is due to other influences, as well as to those of a genuine Mazzinian character.

In estimating the effect that a man has on his own time and on those who come after him, it is not always easy to steer a course between fanatical admiration on the one hand, and an overcautious pedantry, based strictly on documentation, on the other. In Mazzini's case the latter approach might well ignore perhaps the greatest sphere of his influence: that widely diffused atmosphere of inspiration and sympathy that extended far beyond the circle of his immediate following, and of those disciples for whose acceptance of his teaching we have documentary proof.

Read, for instance, the book of reminiscences published in 1910 by the American social worker, Jane Addams, one of those admirable lay saints to be found more frequently in Anglo-Saxon than in Latin society. One morning in 1872, on a farm in Illinois, the little girl, not yet twelve years old, entered her father's room. 'He was sitting by the fire, with a newspaper in his hand, looking very solemn, and upon my eager enquiry what had happened, he told me that Joseph Mazzini was dead. I had never even heard Mazzini's name, and after being told about him I was inclined to grow argumentative, asserting that my father did not know him, that he was not an American, and that I could not understand why we should be expected to feel badly about him. It is impossible to recall the conversation, with the complete breakdown of my cheap arguments, but in the end I obtained that which I have ever regarded as a valuable possession, a sense of the genuine relationship which may exist between men who share large hopes and like desires, even if they differ in nationality, language and creed: that these things count for absolutely nothing between groups of men who are trying to abolish slavery in America or to throw off Hapsburg oppression in Italy. At any rate I was heartily ashamed of my meager notion of patriotism, and I came out of the room exhilarated with the consciousness that impersonal and international relations are actual facts and not mere phrases.'[1] Here was a characteristic instance of Mazzini's influence, on a family of pioneers with anti-slavery views, isolated from the world in the very heart of North America.

Another characteristic instance is described by the American socialist, Dr. Herron.[2] 'Near the community where I was born,' he writes, 'on the Wabash River, founded originally by French Jesuits, there was a Quaker community. I do not remember who among them had a special veneration for Mazzini; but I know that for many of them Mazzini was a sacred character. I could not say when I heard him first spoken of, nor how. I seem always to have known him. He was one of the two or three formative influences in my life, and

[1] Jane Addams: *Twenty Years at Hull-House*, New York, the Macmillan Company, 1920, p. 21.
[2] In a private letter.

I felt as though I knew him personally. I quote my own case, because it is typical of Mazzini's influence in the most unexpected quarters. There was I, a boy far away in a little American community founded by French Jesuits, absorbing the spirit of Mazzini as the bread and wine of my life! And I know other men and women who have told me by chance that they were affected in a similar way.'

The first book on socialism to be published in Japan, by Tomoyoshi Murai, is deeply influenced by the teaching of Mazzini, whom the author considers one of the initiators of the coming social revolution. Sun Yat-Sen, too, the founder of the Chinese Republic, was a fervent admirer of Mazzini, from whom he drew many of his political ideas. The Indian nationalists used Mazzini's biography and translations of his works in making their own propaganda. In an issue of *The Indian Socialist* (November 1912), the nationalist Savarkar, who was threatened with the death penalty by the English courts, was described as 'Mazzini's martyr in India'.

These silent and, as it were, subterranean springs, which gush out after an unknown course, now here, now there, without apparent reason or origin, may even be destined to spread further yet, if mankind is to approach nearer the ideal of social justice dreamed of by Mazzini: even though it may be realized — or realized in part — by the work of men or the use of methods that he would vehemently have disavowed. The further they go, the less they will retain, no doubt, the memory of the distant source from which they are derived; or they will be thought to have other origins. And perhaps this is the greatest victory to be gained by a man's spirit in the course of history: that of becoming diffused in the great sea of Being, there to be most active where it is least known, where perhaps its presence is not even suspected.

If, however, the full extent of Mazzini's indirect influence can never be accurately determined, it is possible to attempt an evaluation of what can be regarded as the solid, central core of his achievement: the direct influence that he had upon the men about him when he was alive, his writings, and the effect that, in its turn, the work of the early Mazzinian disciples had upon their contemporaries.

2

THE FAILURE OF MAZZINI'S RELIGIOUS TEACHING

IN seeking to estimate the effect of Mazzini's religious teaching, we are forced to recognize that even among his closest followers there were very few who fully shared his faith.

According to Mazzini's grandiose plans, the organization entitled *La Giovine Europa* ('Young Europe') was to be a training ground for the 'precursors' and 'apostles' who were to elaborate 'a new philosophy, a new political economy, etc.', in the light of the new faith, and to promote its application to 'all branches of social activity and to the study of language, race and historical origins, so that the mission to be assigned by the new epoch to each of the different peoples may be revealed, and the future order in Europe deduced therefrom'. Together with intellectual renewal, moreover, it was to prepare universal insurrection. But the *Giovine Europa* never succeeded in emerging from its rudimentary state. Its propaganda certainly had a tardy and indirect influence on Swiss constitutional reform in 1848, and served to draw the attention of European democrats to the international character of social and political problems.[1] But apart from these very limited results it had no appreciable effect whatever on the development of nineteenth-century philosophic, scientific or political thought. Scarcely three years after that April day in 1834 when seventeen Germans, Poles and Italians — somewhat audaciously taking upon themselves the representation of their own nations and of the whole world — had met in Berne to found the *Giovine Europa*, Mazzini was forced to admit that it had entirely failed of its purpose. 'It is rumoured abroad', he wrote on August 23rd, 1837, 'that I have deserted the *Giovine Europa*. I have every right to say that the *Giovine Europa* has deserted me. Is there a single one of its signatories who shares my ideas on what it should be? The signatories, I say: so much the worse for them if in signing they misunderstood me or made mental reservations! . . . I have been deceived. I am surrounded today by people who call themselves the *Giovine Europa* and reject all its ideas: by people who only see in it a nominal bond for the purpose of conspiracy, not a band of apostles, a mission, the precursors of a new world. All my ideas and all that I have tried to do are scorned, derided, outraged . . . I stand alone, utterly alone: alone with God, with my memories, with my own faith. And if none shares my faith, am I to blame? Do I abandon, desert, the *Giovine Europa* because your *Giovine Europa* is not mine?'

[1] This was the opinion of Bolton King, who regarded the *Giovine Europa* in other respects as 'pure rhodomontade'. See also Zanichelli, *Politica e storia*, Bologna, Zanichelli, 1903, p. 152.

Later attempts to revive the original organization under the guise of a 'European Centre' during the second half of 1846, and a 'Central Committee of European Democracy' in 1850 and 1855 were equally unfortunate. It is curious to observe the ingenuous way in which Mazzini set about forming committees from which he expected conspicuous results. 'I already have a representative coming from Germany, where he is well-known as a professor and writer; and I am now concerned with Switzerland and other countries,' he wrote on August 2nd, 1846. A month later, 'I have won over the German, who is the man I wanted, Jacoby . . . but I am having difficulties in Switzerland, where Dr. Steiger raises objections.' 'I do not agree with you as to the slight importance of the European meeting, if I succeed. As to having no mandate, that is of no consequence. No one can give us one, because the democratic party has not been constituted . . . What I now need is a Greek, and a Southern Slav from the Austrian Empire' (October 6th, 1846). This habit of Mazzini's of making individual men into an embodiment of their countries has aroused lively criticism.[1]

Among Italians, Mazzini's religious teaching had no success. He realized his own solitary position, which grieved him not only at times when he really was deserted by everyone, but also when he had a considerable number of political adherents. During his imprisonment at Gaeta, in 1870, he wrote: 'I know no

[1] See Montanelli, *Memorie sull'Italia e specialmente sulla Toscana dal* 1814 *al* 1850, Turin, Soc. ed. Italiana, 1853, Preface to 2nd edition.

one in the world at present with whom I could live for more than three days without becoming ungrateful and filled with silent fury. No one knows how disheartened I have been for years: how only my faith in a future I shall never see gives me strength. If I could have my way, I should live in absolute solitude. I have an irresistible need to avoid men, and to be alone with God and the dead.' On April 11th, 1871, he wrote: 'I keep my residence secret from everyone, because I shrink from contact with the Party, which would take up my time and my strength and turn me into a misanthrope in a week or two.' And in June 1871, 'If I let myself be seen, the Party will fall upon me, which would mean I should have no time to myself and should die of rage like a mad dog in a couple of weeks.'

Nor did the Italians who came after him, with certain exceptions, seem better disposed than were his contemporaries to make an effort to understand, far less to adopt, Mazzini's religious revelation in its entirety. Indeed it would seem undeniable that almost all those Italians who claim to be followers of Mazzini are wholly ignorant of Mazzini himself.

His influence as the apostle of a new religion was felt in England rather than in Italy: among radical circles, and particularly by women. Jessie White-Mario and the Signora Crawford-Saffi, transplanted into Italy as the wives of Italians, were among the very few who wholeheartedly accepted the Mazzinian religion.

There were indications of a revival in Italy of Mazzini's religious ideas at the beginning of the present century in the theories of the modernist movement, which had much in common with his. We owe one of the most able and moving commemorative tributes to Mazzini — a Mazzini perhaps not strictly historical because too much Christianized, but presented with a loving understanding of his intimate religious mysticism — to Gallarati-Scotti.[1] And a little book of prayer and of religious *pensées* published with the approval of the ecclesiastical authorities because it contained nothing not strictly orthodox, was also the work of a modernist: for the ecclesiastical censor allowed a passage, signed by the initials G. M.,[2] to escape his notice, unaware of the mistake he was making: a typical case of those silent, subterranean influences, to which we have already referred. But in Italy such instances are rare.

The cultural tradition of Italy contains few romantic elements and is almost exclusively classic. Mazzini's mysticism does not seem suited to, or at least has not yet succeeded in affecting, Italian mental habits. His religion was too political for those who longed for a new faith, and too mystical for those who simply sought freedom for their country; too full of reasoning for the sentimental, and too sentimental for the rational. Far from turning their thoughts to a new religion for Humanity, the Italians had to think of creating their

[1] *Giuseppe Mazzini e il suo idealismo politico*, Milano, Cogliati, 1904. An interesting work by Crespi, *Giuseppe Mazzini e la futura sintesi religiosa*, Florence, Bonducciana, 1912, is also modernist in inspiration.

[2] *L'anima e Dio*, Milano, Tipografia Santa Lega Eucaristica, 1908, 4th edition, pp. 110-11.

own national unity. They had to fight with dogged determination against the tradition of divine right in order to release civil life from all control by the Church and to construct a new lay administration unfettered by pontifical authority. Was it possible for them to accept, in Mazzini's teaching, a theory so profoundly theocratic, and having, beneath its superficial differences, so many points of contact with that other, the evil effects of which they were condemned to endure?

One of the accusations made against Mazzini by his adversaries, and also by his friends when they broke with him, was precisely this: that he wanted to create a despotic theocracy. Giovanni Ruffini wrote, on November 17th, 1837: 'Mazzini thinks he is Pope, and infallible.' Luigi Carlo Farini wrote of him in 1853: 'He is pontiff, prince, apostle, priest. When the clericals have gone, he will be thoroughly at home in Rome.' Felice Orsini called him 'the new Mahomet'; Sirtori would have nothing to do with Mazzinian 'Theo-democracy'; Proudhon accused him of 'wishing to be Pope'; and Marx derisively dubbed him 'Theopompus'.

If the theological postulates upon which Mazzini based his moral and political system are discounted,[1] in other words, if we do not accept the theory that the people's opinion — more reliable than that of any

[1] See Alberto Mario, op. cit., p. 529: 'Mazzini's philosophic and political system proceeds strictly from his theological postulates; if these are taken away, only the most deplorable empiricism is left, which Mazzini has always vigorously combated. Remove God from the formula, and the major term disappears from the syllogism.'

other, whether individual or collective, pontifical or princely — must be the true interpretation of the divine revelation, and that the authority set up by popular suffrage is necessarily the 'true, good, sacred authority' recognized by all and cheerfully obeyed by all; if we do not believe that the collective will can never be led astray, as all others are at times, and that in choosing the nation's representatives universal suffrage will work in a way entirely different from that with which experience has made us familiar, then the whole of Mazzinian democracy falls to the ground. And in fact, the Italian middle class, which bore the responsibility of carrying through the national revolution, had few illusions, indeed had no reason to have any, upon the infallibility of the people. Mazzini's national democratic republic, emanating from a deified people, must have seemed to them simply a new theocracy, likely to be even more oppressive than the old, precisely because it was to have a democratic and elective basis: for those elected by a popular majority would regard themselves as chosen by God and as instruments not so much of a political as a religious mission. They would thus impose their will on the minority with all the intolerance of those who are convinced of being in possession of absolute truth. The minority would oppose the majority in the name not only of their own political principles but in that of their religious creed. All would claim the tradition of Humanity as their own, and would be convinced of having consulted it with the requisite purity of thought and devotion that Mazzini laid down so ingenuously as the criterion of truth. Each would deny to his opponent the right to invoke tradition or to claim that he was fitted to consult it. In other words, since unanimity is impossible, there would be no lack of social and political strife in Mazzini's new order, but it would be complicated and embittered by religious discord.

And after all, Mazzini's Holy Alliance of Peoples was to be constituted — however paradoxical the statement may at first sight appear — not so very differently from Metternich's Holy Alliance of sovereigns. The monarchs of the Holy Alliance proclaimed their belief in God, in Progress (defined according to their own consciences and to the historical tradition that suited them so well) and even in collective humanity. Does not the preamble to the Holy Alliance invoke solidarity among the peoples, the unity of the human family, and the duty of all men to obey God's law upon earth? The princes, too, had a religion of duty, of their own duty; they made great sacrifices in their effort to govern their unruly subjects, who appeared ignorant of the universal moral law as conceived by the princes themselves, in the light of their own consciences and their familiar traditions. Moreover the princes felt the necessity of bringing their actions in the temporal sphere into conformity with the dictates of the spiritual authority residing in Rome. And the Pope, too, was held to be inspired by God. Did not the princes sign their decrees — including those imposing the death penalty — with an invocation for divine help? And was not the suppression of free thought a logical consequence of the mission that the princes regarded as theirs, of educating mankind and leading them unhindered along the way of righteousness? It was only necessary to replace the Pope by the Council of Humanity, and the Kings by the Peoples, for Mazzini's system to emerge complete; the only difference being that universal suffrage would take the place of heredity in the field of politics, and, in that of religion, of election by the cardinals' vote.

It was natural, therefore, that Mazzini's ideal of God and the People should seem a dangerous return to obsolete traditions, an incomprehensible rejection of all the most precious achievements of the liberal movement. In this connection, De Sanctis' lack of comprehension with regard to Mazzini is characteristic. De Sanctis, who was unquestionably the most open-minded Italian liberal of the nineteenth century, and one who appreciated Mazzini's moral and literary importance better than any of those belonging to his own party and his own time, failed to understand either Mazzini's democratic or theocratic beliefs: the doctrine was so alien to his spirit that he, who understood everything, simply could not take it in.

If, in addition, it is remembered that Mazzini, absorbed as he always was in political and revolutionary activities, had no leisure in which to dedicate himself to systematic religious propaganda, and that when at last, towards the end of his life, he was able to do so, men's minds were already dominated by the positivist reaction against early nineteenth-century idealism, the scanty success and indeed almost complete sterility of his religious teaching can well be understood.

3

MAZZINI'S REPUBLICANISM IN THEORY

THE fate of Mazzini's more purely political ideas was happier than that of his religious teaching.

In Mazzini's mind the idea of national unity for Italy was inextricably bound up with that of a republic. He placed both at the head of his programme for the *Giovine Italia* when, as a prisoner in the fortress of Savona, he first planned the movement towards the end of 1830 and the beginning of 1831. He explained the republican character of the new organization by the fact that 'he had just seen the third instance of a prince's treachery occurring in Italy, almost beneath his eyes' (in allusion to that of Ferdinand in 1820, of Carlo Alberto in 1821, and of Francesco of Modena in 1831). But no sooner had he emigrated to France, after his release from prison, than news reached him that Carlo Alberto, 'the conspirator of 1821', had become king; whereupon we see him relegating the republic to the background and stressing the idea of unity. 'All Italy awaits but a word from you,' he wrote in the famous letter addressed to Carlo Alberto, 'a single word to make us yours . . . Place yourself at the head of the nation and write *Union, Liberty and Independence* upon your flag! Be the Napoleon of Italian freedom . . . We shall then rally round you, we shall offer you our lives; we shall unite the lesser states of Italy under your banner . . . Take up this crown: it is yours, if you desire it.'

A few months later, in sending the text of the letter to a friend, he declared that he had no faith whatever in the king: 'He is a coward, if not worse . . . Yet I did not wish the perjured prince to think the voice of liberty was silent. And I wanted to prevent the people from being deceived by a few timid, perfidious concessions.' He gave a similar explanation of the origin of the letter in 1847 and again in 1861. But if such had, in truth, been his intention at the moment of writing, he would hardly have begun with the words: 'If I believed you to be a common king, with a narrow, tyrannical outlook, I would not address you in the language of a free man . . . But you, Sire, are not such a king. Nature, in creating you for the throne, has given you strength of mind and high principles. Italy knows that you have more regal attributes than that of the purple.' Would he have put so much fervour into exhorting Carlo Alberto to choose the path of glory, if he had really, in his heart, believed him to be both cowardly and treacherous? The evidence points to the conclusion that Mazzini, whose early hopes had given way only too soon to disillusionment, had wanted, in later years, to present what had been a sincere and youthful impulse as an act of calculated dissimulation. However this may be, his attitude towards any possible choice that might arise between unity or republic was henceforth clearly defined: if Carlo Alberto were not a coward and a traitor, Mazzini would follow him in the conquest of national unity.

In the second half of 1831, Mazzini founded the *Giovine Italia* ('Young Italy') among the Italian exiles of Marseilles, with an explicit national, democratic and republican programme. The members declared in their printed propaganda that 'they would attempt no alliance with Kings', since it was no longer possible 'to hope for tolerance from princes, or to make agreements not intended to deceive and to screen secret preparations for war'. 'The strongest party is the most logical party: avoid compromises; they are almost always immoral and useless into the bargain.' All the same, the banner of Young Italy bore the words *Liberty*, *Equality*, *Humanity*, *Unity*; but we may seek in vain for that of *Republic*. Its absence is well dealt with by Mazzini in a letter to Sismondi of November 5th, 1832: 'I am republican in my aims for every country, and above all for Italy; but I would adapt myself to a monarchy if, for instance (as is far from probable) a King of Piedmont or of Naples would for this price give us the nucleus of an army and a supply of arms. I want independence, and *therefore I care more for strength than for freedom*; but I would also accept freedom without strength if they were to give it us, because the former would be a very good means of ultimately acquiring the latter, and of knowing how to make use of it.' And at the meeting held at Locarno in March 1833 to organize the expedition to Savoy, the members of Young Italy resolved: 'That a *coup de main* must be carried out in Piedmont to seize the person of His Majesty; if he should not consent, with the Party's approval, to assume leadership of the revolution, he must suffer the fate of Charles X.'

Mazzini was not present at this meeting, but he did not disavow the conspirators' decision. In all probability he considered the idea of Carlo Alberto joining the revolutionary movement as fantastic, and thought it useless to create division among his friends by combating a proposal that must die a natural death. 'To whom can be entrusted the fate of all Italy, the sceptre of the single ruler?' he wrote in the second number of his publication *La Giovine Italia*. 'To one of the present kings? Perish the thought! Only one among them might perhaps have taken the task upon himself. He bore the stain of treachery; but Italy was ready to forget it. The opportunity passed; he would not: and it was as well for us.' In the same issue Jacopo Ruffini, in reference again to Carlo Alberto, wrote: 'When a voice pointed out that he had only to say one word, to win mastery over the whole peninsula, his heart was unmoved, and cowardice prevented his uttering that word of redemption. Twenty million men would have offered him life, liberty and substance; on such a foundation he could have founded the finest throne in the world. But he was not made for such a glorious heritage.' It was necessary, therefore, to be republican. But if the 'far from probable' event had, in fact, come about?

The ruthless repression with which Carlo Alberto responded to the attempts of the *Giovine Italia* destroyed any lingering hopes that the revolutionaries might still have nourished of a monarchical solution to the national problem. All the same, after the raid on Savoy, Mazzini, in writing to Gioberti, made a distinction between theory and practice: in the former 'there must be all the immutability of the law'; in the latter, 'modifications may be necessary', and 'the turn of events may enforce alternative action' (September 15th, 1834). He wrote to Pier Silvestro Leopardi: 'Give up any idea, even for a moment, of compromise, even if it seem a step in the right direction, and be henceforth a republican, openly believing in the necessity and possibility of the triumph of republicanism . . . Nothing is changed in the laws, the aims, and the means that the *Giovine Italia* intends to choose. It insists and will continue to insist on a republican policy, and will refuse any compromise that may be offered' (June 2nd, 1834). But he also wrote to Gaspare Rosales: 'For us the difference lies not in the symbol of republic or monarchy but in the symbol of Italy. Let an Italian province revolt under the leadership of an Italian Napoleon: let it but declare war to the death with Austria, let it proclaim Italian insurrection and unity for Italy under a single crown, and although I may curse them all in my heart and grieve for the Italian initiative and the Italian mission that have come to nothing, I will go and die fighting against the Austrian, under the banner of such an Italian Napoleon' (October 1st, 1834).

The words *Italian mission*, *Italian initiative*, are indications of the new ideas that, owing to contact with Saint-Simon's doctrines, were during these first years of exile taking shape in Mazzini's mind, and, in combination with the early nationalist programme, were in the end to constitute his religious, moral, social and political system.

In this system there is a sharp distinction between a maximum and a minimum programme. The maximum programme set forth a new religious, democratic and republican order for mankind: for a mankind regenerated by the new and perfect divine revelation of which Mazzini regarded himself as the forerunner. The minimum programme was to create an instrument for this great transformation by leading the Italian people, destined by Providence to be the 'Messiah-people' who were to initiate the new phase of history, along the path of democratic freedom and unity in a national republic, and to give them a new religious faith. Their mission was to summon an international religious council in Rome, the city which, for the third time, would become a fount of civilization and a beacon of progress for the human race.

Furthermore, there lies within the minimum programme itself—if the solecism may be forgiven—another, more minimum still. Although, in theory, national unification, an Italian republic, and the new social and religious life of Italy are all treated as of equal importance and are linked indissolubly together in Mazzini's thought, in practice the idea that always takes precedence of the rest is that of the necessity of constituting national and political unity. 'To promote the practical application of our creed we must exist as a united nation.' 'I do not believe that any religious reform can be realized before political reform.' 'Before we can associate with other nations, we must be a nation ourselves. Let us found Italy of the People. Let us acquire our rights as men and citizens. We shall then return with greater dignity, with more hope of being useful and the certainty of not being overborne or betrayed, to the comity of nations.'

During those times when Mazzini could count on no one but himself, he affirmed the complex of his own ideas uncompromisingly, dogmatically, concealing nothing: 'We must show ourselves absolutely as we are; that is, as a religious association whose problem is that of education, and whose subversive work is simply a consequence of the principle of action in every possible way' (1837); '*Je ne transigerai plus d'une seule ligne avec personne, parce que tout est inutile, sauf de vivre et de mourir fidèles à nos convictions*' (1838); 'We must, more than ever, be exclusively Young Italians' (1844, after the death of the Bandiera brothers); and in 1853, after the rising in Milan, he wrote: 'I have just sent a few lines telling them to save ink and postal expenses, since I will accept neither proposals nor correspondence from a committee that is not republican, and shall fight to the death against retrograde ideas.' '*The less you hope for immediate results, the more absolute you must be*;

compromise may sometimes be necessary on the eve of action, but not in the teaching of principles' (1858). 'I no longer work for anything but the overthrow of the monarchy: there is no other way of regaining Rome, of conquering the Trentino, of remedying the economic ills of our country and the still deeper wounds that are daily inflicted upon our honour and dignity' (1868).

But so soon as there appears a possibility, however remote, of national unity being achieved without a new religion, without democracy or a republic, he finds in the very unshakable nature of his own faith, the strength not to be intransigent; convinced that time will, sooner or later, complete his work, he postpones the full realization of his programme to the future, puts everything else aside, and concentrates all his strength upon the conquest of Italian unity with Rome as the nation's capital.

He gives up testifying to his own faith when, in so doing, he might injure the national cause. 'I have no right', he wrote in 1838, 'to embarrass the movement, in the name of an exclusive religious creed. When the day for action dawns, the *Giovine Italia* will ascertain its own religious beliefs. If they are not the true faith they will do little harm and be but short-lived.' At Milan, in June 1848, he joined in the Corpus Domini procession; when Triumvir of the Roman Republic in 1849 he allowed Catholicism to be declared the state religion in the plan for the Constitution, and, with the other authorities, attended the Easter celebrations in Saint Peter's. Later he intervened to prevent confessionals from the churches being used as barricades. Giuseppe Ferrari and Alberto Mario blamed Mazzini for thus rendering homage to Catholicism; but they were wrong to do so, for in such actions he was not forgetful of his own religious ideals, indeed, he believed that, in avoiding spiritual discord, he brought them a step nearer, and made possible the defence of Rome.

Mazzini was also ready to set his social and democratic ideas aside until national unity could be achieved. 'No one in Italy, whether worker or no, can freely express his own ideas; no one can attempt to do so. The press is a monopoly not of a class but of the governments. And behind the seven Italian governments, all of them more or less openly enemies to freedom of opinion, stands Austria, the enemy of every government or people, of every class and every thought, of all, in fact, that is Italian in name or semblance. Before the worker can complain that freedom has not bettered his lot, the nation itself must exist; the seven governments and Austria must be overthrown.' 'The first and foremost of your duties', Mazzini tells the workers, 'is that which you owe your country. You must constitute Italy; it is a simple necessity.' 'Without a country you have no name, no vote, no rights, no baptism of brotherhood among the peoples. You are humanity's bastards. Soldiers without a flag, Israelites among the nations, you will win neither trust nor protection: none will be your sureties. Do not imagine that you can free yourselves from unjust social conditions before winning a country for yourselves. Do not be seduced by the idea of improving your material conditions without first solving the national question: you cannot succeed. Only your own land, the great, fertile land of Italy, stretching from the Alps to the furthest shores of Sicily, can bring your hopes to fruition.'

It is interesting to see how Mazzini put this theory into practice immediately after the Five Days in Milan. On April 3rd and 4th, 1848, there were 'meetings of workers in the tailoring trades, who wanted to form unions for the purpose of making certain claims for an increase in wages, for the prohibition of Sunday work and the closing of second-hand clothes' shops'. The *Lombardo*, a paper run by followers of Mazzini, printed the following statement on April 5th: 'Among us, too, the workers are imitating their brothers in France, England and Germany, and are uniting to demand an increase in pay. We, who are fighting for the people's rights, liberties and independence, hope to be worthy of their trust and therefore to be believed when we tell them that such gatherings, such demonstrations, are at the present time inopportune. The workers are quite right: their wages ought to be brought into relation with their work and their needs, and we shall uphold their rights so soon as the appropriate moment comes. But now it is necessary for all citizens to unite in driving the Austrians from Italy. Once this has been accomplished and we are secure in our independence, then our chief care will be to see that the workers are not cheated of the fruits of their labour.'

As to the republic, Mazzini had no faith in the

achievement of unity in any other way, since he could not believe that any of the Italian princes were capable of desiring or of obtaining the crown of a united Italy; and for this reason he ceaselessly preached the necessity of rising against them all and of creating a national republic. 'We are against the monarchy,' he wrote, characteristically, 'not because we are republicans but because we stand for national independence.' And from the necessity of fighting against all the royal houses in order to set up national unity sprang the need to appeal for support to the working classes, who were eager for a better social order. Thus even in the practical field the different parts of his theory seemed to him indissoluble.

But so soon as he begins to speculate on the share that an 'Italian Napoleon' might have in achieving the unification of Italy, he does not hesitate to make his position clear. 'We stand, before all else, for national unity, and if we are offered some other way, more speedy and secure than ours, of attaining it, we shall know how to remain silent, and, keeping our faith in its future triumph unchanged in our hearts, we shall rally in concord round the new banner.' 'I am, and ever was and ever shall be, before all else, a supporter of national unity.' 'The republic can wait, but not national unity.' 'I am only concerned for the unification of Italy.'[1]

[1] Mazzini's mental attitude towards the problem of national unity and a republic appears in its most characteristic form during the years 1846-47; see Salvemini, '*Giuseppe Mazzini dall'aprile* 1846 *all'aprile* 1848', in the *Raccolta di studi storici in onore di Giacinto Romano,* Pavia, 1907.

4

MAZZINI'S REPUBLICANISM IN PRACTICE

WHEN Mazzini turned from the preaching of abstract principles to the sphere of action, he at once assumed an attitude of political neutrality that affords a curious contrast with his previous intransigence. 'We shall say nothing,' he declared, for instance, in some written instructions (it would seem, of January 1844) for the organization of a great insurrection which, as usual, did not take place, 'We shall say nothing about decreeing a republic; nor will others decree a monarchy. Once the whole of Italy is freed, from the sea to the Alps, a national council elected by universal suffrage will decide her destiny, but not before. While the state of insurrection persists, all opinions will be allowed legal expression, except such as would deny freedom, national unity and independence.'

In 1850 his position was the same. 'So long as our work remains that of preaching the new faith, we believe it our duty never to compromise. We shall therefore continue with all possible ardour to preach the necessity for national unity and a republic. But in passing from the field of education to that of action, we become aware of fresh duties: duties towards the Italian people, towards the nation that today is still unable to give expression to its will. When it can do so, its sovereignty will be our law. We have no intention, even if we had the power to do so, of imposing a republic or any other form of government upon the people by force. The war must be directed by a body with exceptional powers. Once Italian territory is freed, the Nation will speak and we shall obey.' In 1853, at a meeting held at Lugano to prepare for the rising in Milan on February 6th, Mazzini again declared that 'what he wanted was a free and united Italy, and he believed that only a republic could make her so; but that he respected the hopes and opinions of others who put their trust in a constitutional Piedmont'. He added these precise words: 'At the news that Milan has risen, either the King and the moderate party will decide to come and repeat the attempt of 1848, and we shall receive them with open arms: or they will not intervene, and the people and the army will join us without them, since it would be impossible for Piedmont to remain an idle spectator of such an event. We must therefore abstain from proclaiming a republic or any other form of government; but we must set up a provisional government simply to direct the war and to call all Italy to arms.' The provisional government should be formed of 'men of both parties' and Mazzini expressly did not include himself. In 1856, 'when it seemed probable that a strong concerted attempt at insurrection would be made in Sicily and Naples before the year was out, Mazzini and Garibaldi, Cosenz and Crispi together with Fabrizi, all agreed to keep silent on the political programme, and simply to stress the unification and independence of the Italian nation'.

The Italians, therefore — Mazzini always counted those ready for instant insurrection in millions — were to rise all together and, with irresistible force, to fall upon the Austrians. The ruling princes of Italy were to be overwhelmed with the foreigner; if any showed a wish to join in the anti-Austrian crusade, they were to be allowed to do so; but until the enemy was defeated, Italy's future political order was to remain undecided. Republicans and monarchists were to wage war in brotherly union, but they could continue, in private, peacefully to propagate their own ideas — on the understanding that everyone preached national unification — and they were all to wait patiently for the sovereign people, inspired by God, finally to give its answer. They were not to concern themselves as to how matters were, in the end, to turn out, and were above all to resist the temptation of taking any precautionary measures whatever against the possibility that the people might be mistaken in their decision and not truly inspired by God; in other words, that they might appear to think differently from the way in which one side or the other would wish them to think.

It was a fantastic plan. Mazzini himself was not so ingenuous as to take his own Utopia entirely seriously. He assumed an attitude of neutrality in order not to discourage such monarchists as might be willing to join in the revolt and who hoped that intervention by the ruling princes might tilt the balance in favour of a monarchical policy. But he was convinced that no such intervention would ever take place, and that when it came to the point the disappointed monarchist patriots, too, would support a republican programme.

In 1848, when the insurrection of the Five Days had taken place and Carlo Alberto had joined in the national war against Austria, Mazzini hastened from London to Milan, protesting that he wanted only victory over the Austrians, and was willing to accept whatever regime the nation decided on, when the war was over. He made every effort to induce the moderates in the Lombard Provisional Government to speed up the arming of volunteers and to intensify military operations. He genuinely wanted first and foremost the defeat of the Austrian forces, even if it were to redound to the credit of Carlo Alberto and the moderate party. But in his own heart he was sure that the King, sooner or later, would fail the patriots, and that the moderates would reveal themselves as unequal to the task. In his exhortations to battle could be discerned the indictment he was preparing against the allies of the day who were to become the enemies of the morrow. Meanwhile he was secretly working for a republican democratic rising to take place as soon as the King and the Provisional Government were wholly discredited.

For their part, the moderates in the Provisional Government, who had nothing to learn from Mazzini in the exercise of guile, also declared in their manifestoes and official documents that when the war was over the nation should pronounce upon its own fate; but they secretly urged Carlo Alberto to promote the fusion of Lombardy with Piedmont, if necessary by means of a *coup d'état*, since they were anxious to assure themselves, with the King's help, of ascendancy in the new regime to the exclusion of the democrats. Thus they obstructed the arming of the volunteers by every possible means, for fear that the latter would merely serve to reinforce the democratic party. Carlo Alberto, too, declared that he had come as a brother to the assistance of brothers, and would put off the consideration of all political questions until the war was won; but, ever fearful of a republican revolution, he dared not throw all his forces into the war against Austria, gave only weak support to the insurgents at Venice who had proclaimed a republic, and thought chiefly of securing control of Lombard territory. Thus the political truce merely served to mask a secret struggle between all parties, and at the same time paralysed any serious attempt at military action. When, in the end, the truce was broken and the moderates supported a plebiscite for fusion with Piedmont, accusations of disloyalty and bad faith broke out on every hand. It was Radetzki who carried off the victory: for he drove Carlo Alberto out of Lombardy, brought the moderates to heel, and destroyed Mazzini's dreams of a national republic.

In reality, there were only two possible solutions for the national problem: either a general insurrection against Austria must be carried out with all the ruling princes of Italy hostile to it, which would necessitate, from the start, the proclamation of a republic; or one of the princes would take part whole-heartedly in the liberation and unification of Italy, in which case the republicans would from the beginning have to leave a way open to his triumph, unless they intended to reward their ally for his patriotic action by sending him about his business at the moment of victory.

The long-awaited opportunity for a general rising never occurred again, after the ill-fated attempt of 1848. All Mazzini's efforts to promote one ended in failure and in ruthless repression by the authorities, which kept national sentiment and hatred for the existing regime alive, but was disastrous from the point of view of the republican cause. On the other hand, after the Congress of Paris in 1856, and throughout all the succeeding complicated series of events, the House of Savoy's participation in the national cause appeared to be assured.

Faced by this new and unexpected situation, Mazzini at first maintained a hostile attitude, suspecting that it would lead to nothing but waste of time. He urged his friends to have no illusions and to hold themselves in readiness to carry out a popular insurrection so soon as the impotence of the House of Savoy in solving the national problem became clear to all. But when the war of 1859 broke out, and intervention by the Piedmontese monarchy in the work of liberation appeared irrevocable, Mazzini little by little abandoned both the rigidity of his preaching and his former strict political neutrality, and assumed an attitude of active, if mistrustful co-operation. In other words, although not concealing his own lack of faith in the ultimate success of a venture that in his opinion was based on insecure foundations — since he was always of the opinion that the House of Savoy would never carry through the task of achieving complete Italian national unity — he gave up his republican propaganda, bowed his head before the monarchy on the understanding that it was to take the lead in the struggle for independence, and associated his own efforts with those of the monarchists, although ready to raise the republican banner once more if they should meet with failure. 'The republicans of the party of action are not plotting for a republic. When, before the last war, we saw Italy mistakenly following in the footsteps of the monarchy, we kept our own faith to ourselves, furled the republican flag, and helped every party, upon whatever side, that seemed directed, from however great a distance, towards the sacred goal of national unity. The men of republican faith were silent, believing in the urgent necessity for all forces in the country to be concentrated on achieving unity in the way pointed out by the majority; but they kept, and keep themselves, free to take another road when it becomes evident that the present one does not lead to the chosen goal.' 'Thirty-four years ago I pledged my faith to a united and republican Italy. I kept silent when the whole country thought otherwise and decided to try another way.' 'Our programme of *Italian republican unity* dates from a third of a century ago: we have never proclaimed it when it was necessary for a misguided people to learn its truth through experience and disillusionment.'

Finally, in the last months of 1863 and the beginning of 1864, it would seem that Mazzini really thought the national cause would benefit if he co-operated with Victor Emmanuel in the liberation of the Veneto and the war against Austria. He had no hesitation then in defying the objections of those friends, who, as Saffi said, 'clinging to the principle of republicanism, refused all contact with the monarchy, even in matters of national importance transcending by far the political question of the form that the future state was to take'; and he entered into negotiations with the King, prolonging them until he had lost all hope of reaching any useful agreement.

5

MAZZINI AND THE OTHER REPUBLICANS

WHEN Mazzini suspended his republican propaganda or went so far as to negotiate with the King for the purpose of combining their efforts, he was always careful to make it perfectly clear that he reserved to himself full freedom of action for the future: since the necessity for a new order, not merely national but also republican, social and religious, and not only in Italy but throughout the world, was in his eyes based upon reasons that were absolute and permanent, transcending the inevitably mutable nature of events. 'Our republican faith must remain unshaken through all the vicissitudes of political life, although in the sphere of action it may sometimes be expedient not to press for its immediate realization' (1859). 'The greatest sacrifice I ever made was when, in the cause of unity and civil concord, I gave up preaching my faith and declared that out of respect, not for ministers or monarchists, but for a majority — it mattered little whether mistaken or not — of the Italian people, I would accept the Monarchy and was ready to cooperate with it, provided that the foundations of Italian unification were thereby laid; and that if I felt in duty bound one day to raise our former banner again, I would loyally and publicly inform both my friends and enemies. I can make no other sacrifice, of my own accord' (1860). 'I bow my head in sorrow to the national will, but I shall be no servant or retainer of the monarchy: and the future will show whether my faith rests on the Truth or no' (1861). 'I cannot and will not bind myself for the future' (1864). 'I gave my support, as seemed to me right, and in so far as I was able, to all that could contribute towards solving the first part of the problem: but without ever, as others did, converting what should only remain for us a temporary expedient, into an absolute principle' (1867). 'We have never abandoned our programme.'

It was an equivocal position, and very difficult to maintain. Mazzini himself failed at times to keep it up, and allowed words to escape him that belied his real opinions. For instance, when he compared the two ideas of national unity and republicanism, he sometimes forgot that republicanism was, according to his own theories, a religious, moral and social principle, and treated it simply as a political form not necessary to national unity. 'There is no question here of political forms; there is no question of a republic or a monarchy' (December 31st, 1847). 'Our first thought must be for the war: our second for the unity of the nation; our third for the *form*, the institution that must assure the people of their liberty and their mission' (May 13th, 1848). 'We do not intend to impose a republic or any other form of government by force' (1850). 'We want national unity and freedom for Italy. We are not concerned with political forms' (1860). 'Has there ever, in any part of Italy, been a single attempt at a republican rising? Have we ever, from the earliest days of the movement in Italy, raised the question of the form her political institutions were to take? No; and let whoever has proof to the contrary give me the lie' (1860). 'We stand aside [from the monarchy] not because we insist on any form of political institution, which is simply a question of logic, but in order not to substitute the political for the national question' (1863).

It is true that these are merely statements made, so to speak, in passing, and should not be taken too seriously. But if Mazzini himself found it difficult to keep his foothold upon the razor's edge to which he had committed his steps, it was far more arduous for his followers to maintain their balance and not to slip towards one side or the other.

For instance, in the second half of 1849, Alberto Mario wrote as follows: 'Brother republicans, let us keep our political faith and the right to preach it pacifically, but let us hasten loyally to take up arms under the leadership of Victor Emmanuel: it is our duty.' Aurelio Saffi said much the same thing in May 1860. Mazzini would have been careful not to compromise himself in such a way, and in May 1860 he wrote to Saffi gently reproving him for his attitude. 'I fear you have gone too far, in the party's name, in renouncing our freedom of action and placing it in Victor Emmanuel's hands. We make no renunciation: we *accept* the will of the Italian people. We do not cry *long live Victor Emmanuel*, and enforce his will in Sicily or anywhere else. We cry, *Freedom and unity*. We will bow the head to the other cry when it comes from the people in arms. This is our line, and we must not forsake it.' In October 1861 there was a further move towards the monarchy by Saffi, and Mazzini again wrote to recall him to his former allegiance. 'I know of his intentions,' he wrote to Giorgina Saffi, 'but I believe him to be wrong, and the others with him, in deviating from us. He certainly cannot accuse me of rabid and intolerant republicanism; but on the other hand we have to steer a middle course [between uncompromising republicanism and support of the monarchy] as men who have agreed to make an experiment and are prosecuting it loyally, but are doubtful of its outcome and who therefore behave in such a way as to be able one day to say to their fellow-citizens, if the country's salvation should demand it, *did we not tell you so?* It was with Aurelio's agreement that I said [in 1860]: Either with you or without you, or against you if you cannot give us Rome, or if you surrender our nation, etc. We must keep to this position, and I have never departed from it. But to speak as he has about the Statute, and then to put forward that curious proposition, that the nation cannot make Italy without the Monarchy; to pledge himself not only to Victor Emmanuel but to his legitimate descendants; this is, in truth, too much, it is passing outright from one camp to another. If it be so, I would deplore it from the moral point of view, and from the intellectual I should regard it as an error . . . It would grieve me, too, I cannot say how deeply, on the score of our former friendship and for many other reasons, if Aurelio were to let himself be attracted into the camp of the *doctrinaires*.'

Disagreement increased in the years that followed. 'The fact is that you are all, consciously or unconsciously, in a false position, deceived by empty formulae that leave Italy at the mercy of men who only embroil you with one another . . . You may think yourselves fortunate in the future that Farini and Minghetti will give you, rather than Rattazzi' (October 7th, 1862). 'Aurelio seeks the impossible . . . Greet Aurelio from me, shaking your head in reproof, on my behalf' (January 23rd, 1863). 'Remember me to Aurelio although he is in a different camp' (April 18th, 1863). 'But our ways diverge at all points. Therefore mutual silence is inevitable, but the reasons for it grieve me deeply' (May 1863). 'In very truth, however much I resolve to keep silent with all you political ex-friends of mine, I cannot help myself. If there is anything that drives me almost out of my wits, it is your attitude' (August 21st, 1863). Even Federico Campanella let slip the statement, during a meeting at Genoa in March 1862, that 'we all want Italy, one and indivisible, with Victor Emmanuel as a constitutional King.'

It was worse, naturally, for those who, though adhering to Mazzini's movement, not only were not in constant touch with him but who did not wholly share his opinions. Very few members of his party, as we have already seen, accepted his religious system or even knew it thoroughly. Each one took what he liked from the mass of the Master's writings and neglected or failed to understand the rest. Unity, republic, the people, God, duty, Italy's mission, the Third Rome, taken singly and apart from their context, were repeated by his followers in a sense that differed from, or was entirely opposed to, that of the original doctrine. While Mazzini looked on the republic as a religious and social institution willed by God, the majority of his followers were republicans simply because they despaired of any prince in Italy upholding the cause of freedom and unity after the defeat of Austria and the lesser ruling houses. Although more or less democratic in their sentiments, many of them did not follow the Master in his social teaching, or go so far as to desire, with him, a new economic order without inequality or a wage-earning class. The lack of understanding between Mazzini and the Bandiera brothers was characteristic: the former could not conceive of a revolutionary movement without the people's participation, which, to the latter, trained in the Austrian forces, was not to be thought of.

The heterogeneous nature of Mazzini's party did not escape its contemporaries. After 1846, Cavour, with the keen observation and sound common sense which were the hallmark of his genius, had written: 'A democratic revolution in Italy has little likelihood of success. In proof of this we have only to analyse the elements composing the party that favours political change. This party does not arouse much sympathy with the mass of the people, which except in a very few urban centres is in general attached to the ancient institutions of the country. Its support comes almost exclusively from the middle class and a part of the upper class. But both of these have many interests to preserve and defend. In Italy the ownership of property is not, thank Heaven, the exclusive privilege of any one class. Even where a feudal nobility still remains, it shares with the third estate in ownership of the land. The subversive doctrines of the *Giovine Italia* can have little hold on classes so strongly interested in maintaining the present social order. For this reason — apart from the young, in whom experience has not yet modified the beliefs absorbed in the too stimulating atmosphere of school and college — it can be affirmed that there are in Italy only a very small number of persons who seriously wish to put into practice the extravagant ideas of a group that has become embittered by misfortune. If our social order were really threatened, if the great principles on which it rests were in very truth endangered, many among the most determined opponents of the regime, among even the most hot-headed republicans, would, we are persuaded, very soon be found in the ranks of the conservative party.' And Giovanni Ruffini, recounting in 1853 the origins of the Young Italy movement, wrote as follows: 'The choice of a republican symbol met with little or no opposition. There was no acceptable candidate at that time in Italy for a constitutional monarchy. The past of all the petty princes of Italy was so bad and so anti-national that no reasonable person would ever have thought of offering one of them the Italian crown. This accounts for the fact that republicanism encountered so little opposition among the original members of the association. But all those who accepted it were not convinced republicans. On the contrary, many of them would have preferred a constitutional monarchy, and only accepted a republican policy because they could see no possibility of any other form of government being set up. Others cared only for the independence of Italy, in return for which they were ready to adapt themselves to any kind of regime.' 'A republican party, in the true sense of the word, did not exist,' explained Alberto Mario. 'It was simply a party of action, composed of republicans who dedicated themselves to the liberation of Italy in favour of the monarchy that shared in the enterprise.'

Such a party was bound to disintegrate when Pius IX in 1846, Carlo Alberto in 1848, and Victor Emmanuel after the Congress of Paris showed themselves willing to play a part in the work of national liberation. A few strict and inflexible republicans refused to co-operate; others, with Mazzini, although suspecting a trap, ended by joining forces with the monarchy to achieve a common aim, while preserving their faith intact;[1] but the majority forgot all about republicanism,

[1] Guerrazzi, *Scritti politici*, Milano, Guigoni, 1862, p. 794: 'The democratic

democracy and revolution, and became ardent monarchists.

It was wrong to regard such defection as apostasy. It was due not only to the hopes raised by the monarchy but also to the lack of success that had attended the attempts of the Mazzinians. Theory is all very well, but when, as De Sanctis observes, the teacher has to convince not a class of students but a whole people, it is usually success alone that counts.

Thus we see the republican party being formed and gaining strength between 1831 and 1834, after the monarchy's unfortunate experience with the Carbonari, and during a time when the ruling princes were most anti-national in their outlook and most supine in their devotion to Austrian interests. It completely broke up after the Savoy expedition; was re-constituted in the second half of 1839, when the state of international politics made it possible to raise the Italian question again without any of the rulers appearing likely to exploit the situation as yet in their own interest, and was gravely shaken and discredited — to the advantage of the moderate party — after the disastrous expedition of the

parties have sweated blood for the regeneration of Italy: if they opposed the princes, it was because the latter were devouring the country like wild beasts . . . The democrats suffered, struggled, forestalled events, and seemed ready to act alone and against the principate: but all that was nothing; the moment the opportunity of raising Italy up presented itself, the democrats approached the constitutional monarchy, and with it and for it, fought Italy's battles.' Bertani, in J. White Mario, *Agostino Bertani e i suoi tempi*, I, 285: 'How often are the firmest convictions, founded on hard experience and stern reasoning, suddenly dazzled by a tempting announcement! It is then that we, old Italian patriots, stoop like lovers, in our own despite, to hasty agreements: forget our intentions, matured by suffering; and gladly condone past injury and deception. As long as we are given a good war, and the needful weapons, against the enemy from without, we shall always be found, blind and forgetful, in the front ranks.'

Bandiera brothers. It remained almost without adherents between 1846 and 1848, after the princes had undertaken internal reforms and were manifesting a national spirit; recovered after the Allocution of April 29th, the May risings and the Salasco armistice; and accomplished prodigies in 1849 at Venice and Rome. Subsequently it kept going for some years, with the prestige acquired in 1849, but was greatly weakened by the *coup d'état* of December 2nd, 1851, when Louis Napoleon destroyed the republic in France and with it any hope of an easy republican revolution in Italy. It was nearly ruined by the unfortunate attempt in Milan on February 6th, 1853; it disappeared almost completely after the Crimean war, and particularly during the early part of 1859; and it made an unexpected recovery after the armistice of Villafranca, though it still did not oppose the monarchy, indeed, it formed under Garibaldi's leadership the most resolute and ardent section of the Action Party. After the September convention it gained in strength, and continued to do so after the disastrous war of 1866 and the Mentana defeat, because Napoleon III refused to allow the monarchical government to occupy Rome; and it was on the point of gaining the upper hand in September 1870. As national unity was won, step by step, and finally, with the capture of Rome, completed, very many former republicans gave their allegiance to the monarchy, as the institution that in the nature of things had become identified with national unity. Thus sooner or later they came to agree more or less with what Carducci was to write in 1882: 'If the Italian people, persuaded that Italy could not be unified without the monarchy, called in the House of Savoy, was it the fault of the House of Savoy? The historical and political ambitions of the dynasty would probably have been confined to northern Italy; it was we, we ourselves, with Giuseppe Mazzini at our head, who dragged it into central Italy; Garibaldi won the South for it, and won it over, in the South. If, then, thanks to the malleable nature of the human animal, which enables it to personify its ideals in order to worship or vituperate them as suits it best, the head of the House of Savoy now represents Italy and the State, let us cry, Long live Italy! Open wide the doors and we will enter in to bow before the King!'[1]

Carducci's case is a typical instance of the misunderstandings between Mazzini and the other republicans. 'The year 1860', wrote Carducci, 'left me a democratic monarchist; 1870 found me a republican.' But Carducci's opportunist, free-thinking and classical republicanism had nothing in common with the absolute, mystical and romantic republicanism of Mazzini. And it is a curious fact that, so far as is known, there is no mention whatever of Carducci in any of Mazzini's works or correspondence; although Carducci, in the last years of Mazzini's life, was an outstanding figure

[1] See Alberto Mario, op. cit., p. 527: 'The flower of the parliamentary Left was composed of Mazzinians, who carried their master's principles out to their ultimate conclusions, and with strict logic turned from conspiracies and insurrection in the cause of national unity, to entering the Chamber of Deputies in order to give it form and life.'

in the republican party and cannot have escaped his notice. Probably Mazzini, realizing the abyss that divided him from the poet — and who knows how deeply he must have been shocked by the *Inno a Satana*! — always avoided speaking of him, as was his habit with those whom he disliked.

6

MAZZINI AND THE UNITY OF ITALY

IN 1847 Mazzini evaluated the fruits of his own work as amounting to one-fifth of what his movement had hoped. He could not have made a different estimate after 1870.

To produce even this fifth, other forces that were not in sympathy with his own thought and action had powerfully contributed. In so complex a system of cause and effect as that of the Italian Risorgimento, it would be ingenuous to attribute responsibility to Mazzini for the whole of the results achieved.

Many other writers had played their part with Mazzini in fostering now one, now another, of the elements that go to make up Italian national sentiment. From this point of view, not only Dante, Petrarch and Machiavelli, but Alfieri, Foscolo, Manzoni, indeed, all Italian literature down the centuries, had prepared the minds of Italians for the conquest of unity. But so far as practical action was concerned, it is certain that Mazzini, during his years of exile, was ill-informed on the real conditions of the country in which he was to operate; he was too ready to deceive himself as to the millions of men ready to join in brotherly insurrection — Giovanni Ruffini had good reason to christen him Fantasio in his novel *Lorenzo Benoni* — and too prone to despise the slow, cautious, cool-headed nature of the diplomacy on which, nevertheless, it was necessary to rely in an eminently international problem like that of Italy. He was, moreover, averse to any concession whatever on the ideal of national unity which represented the irreducible minimum of his own aspirations, but which to others must often have seemed remote and fantastic. Thus Mazzini unquestionably lacked many qualities that are indispensable in a leader who passes from the preaching of ideas to their practical application through a great political movement. And if Garibaldi had not been the right arm of the national party, as Mazzini was its soul; if Cavour and his successors, with all the conservative party, had not, in their steady support of the Piedmontese monarchy, intervened again and again — turning the results of the national movement to their own advantage, but at the same time consolidating them and procuring them the reluctant sanction of other governments — it would be very difficult to say whether, or to what extent, Mazzini's national 'apostolate' would have been realized at all.

Nor should the work of his disciples, of the fighting men and the statesmen blind us to what was, in reality, the principal factor in the Italian Risorgimento: the anonymous, collective action of those various groups of liberals who were not pledged to any one leader or party, and who with their good sense, their unheroic but able opportunism, knew when to wait and when to take risks, when to protest and when to be silent, how to *reculer pour mieux sauter* and how to combine their efforts, however diverse, in action that seems to us today, from a distance, so admirably well-balanced and co-ordinated.

Finally, it is undeniable that there had been many others, before Mazzini, who had wished to see an Italy no longer dismembered, no longer forgetful of her ancient glory and a pawn in the game to the ambitions of her neighbours. Recent research, although it has eliminated from the ranks of true prophets of Italian unity and independence Dante, Petrarch and all those lesser writers hailed by our fathers as patriots of the Risorgimento if they so much as introduced the name of Italy into their works, has on the other hand revealed the existence of a rich vein of openly national sentiment in the troubled period of French conquest, from 1796 to 1814. These theories, however, of a united Italy, clothed in republican trappings in the early days of Jacobin conquest, and carefully presented in monarchical guise under the Napoleonic despotism, are confined, as Masi observes, merely to the book or pamphlet, or individual aspirations, of some particular poet or patriot; they are Arcadian laments, classical reminiscences, scholastic exercises, vague projects with no plan of execution, or at the most uncoordinated ventures followed by swift disillusionment. With the fall of the Napoleonic Empire and the Treaty of

Vienna, the unity of Italy seemed to vanish for ever into the region of dreams. A few references to it can be found in some obscure Carbonaro literature of the years between 1815 and 1831. But from 1815 to 1860 it was firmly believed by all sensible people that the political unification of Italy, whether in a monarchical or republican form, was — to quote Cesare Balbo's words in 1843 — 'A puerile idea, held at the most by pettifogging students of rhetoric, common rhymesters and café politicians.'[1]

Giuseppe Mazzini, on the other hand, believed the unification of Italy to be not only possible but necessary. He insisted upon it with single-minded obstinacy, and dedicated his whole life to realizing this ideal, from his early, ardent youth to his grief-stricken old age. He preached it incessantly, in the face of ridicule, disappointment and defeat; communicated his own faith to others simply by virtue of being all the more unshaken in his convictions, the more it seemed that facts were against him; and he doggedly opposed any other solution of the problem, clinging desperately to his own faith even when everything appeared to counsel a more limited and practical outlook. He, and he alone, was responsible for that psychological preparation which, between 1856 and 1860, brought to nothing the manœuvres of those Italian liberals who would have accepted a Murat on the throne of Naples, thereby replacing a divided Italy under Austrian domination

[1] *Delle speranze d'Italia*, Le Monnier's edition of 1885, pp. 28 and 289, n. 1; Tivaroni, *L'Italia durante il dominio Austriaco*, Turin, L. Roux e C., 1892-94, pp. 500 et seqq.

by an Italy, still divided, but dominated by France; that psychological preparation from which in 1859 sprang the annexations in Central Italy, in 1860 the expedition of the Thousand, and in 1862 and 1867, Aspromonte and Mentana: from which, in a word, sprang Italian unity. It was Mazzini and Mazzini alone, who imposed upon the Italian liberal-nationalist groups the one dominating idea, to which, through all the vicissitudes of the making of Italy, everything else was to become subordinated.

7

ANALOGIES BETWEEN MAZZINI'S TEACHING AND SOCIALISM

WHILE in Italy men's minds were preoccupied with the mainly political problem of achieving national status for their country, abroad, and above all in France and England — highly developed capitalist countries, already in possession of complete national independence and of representative government — the first class-struggles between *bourgeoisie* and proletariat were being staged, and socialist theories, the seeds of which had already appeared in the revolutionary philosophy of the eighteenth century, were in process of development. Even in Italy, despite the censorship and police surveillance, foreign, and particularly French socialist theories had penetrated to a greater extent than is usually believed, and flourished side by side with the indigenous growth of the older so-called 'Utopian' socialist ideas. But for a long time they came up against the victorious competition of Mazzinian propaganda.

Not that Mazzini's theories were always in conflict with the entire complex of economic, social and moral ideas that went under the name of socialism in the nineteenth century. Four-fifths of Mazzini's ideas were Saint-Simonist in origin. Many of the theories that in the second half of the century became the heritage of the socialist parties, were at first common to all supporters of democracy. And if, for instance, we take those that, after being roughly outlined during the eighteenth century and elaborated in the writings of the democrats and 'Utopians' of the first half of the nineteenth, were finally detached from the rest and organized into the Marxist system, we find that in many points the Mazzinian system agrees with the Marxist, or at least includes principles that, carried to their logical conclusion, as Bolton King pointed out, would make them end in Marxism.[1]

Common to both Mazzinianism and Marxist socialism is a belief in the growing, beneficent social and political power of the working-classes, 'the principal new element' in history. 'The rise of the artisan classes in the cities dates now from more than a century ago: slow and tenacious in its progress, and proceeding from decade to decade according to the law of accelerated motion, it has grown visibly in intensity and extent during the last twenty years, becoming organized and conscious of genuine power.' 'The people appears upon the scene, and does not intend to allow a second aristocracy, even if a different and more numerous one, to replace the first. Thus the struggle little by little

[1] Op. cit. pp. 297, 308. Saffi, too, in his Preface to the writings of Mazzini indicates similarities between Mazzinianism and Marxist socialism that are entirely lacking between Mazzinianism and the old forms of communism that had continued in anarchism. See Cantimori, op. cit., pp. 322-3.

changes its aspect, and whereas it formerly lay between one class and another it now lies between the class-principle and the principle of equality, between privilege and labour.'

Common, too, to both systems, is the belief that the proletariat has specific interests to promote and that for this reason class organization is necessary. 'In Italy', wrote Mazzini in 1844, 'there are two classes of men, as everywhere else: those who have exclusive possession of the elements of all labour, that is to say, land, credit or capital; and the others, who own nothing but their hands . . . The first, who are fettered in the use of their faculties, despised by their foreign oppressors, and subjected to the arbitrary rule of bad and stupid princes, need a political revolution; the second, crushed by poverty, harassed by precarious work and inadequate wages, are chiefly in need of a better social order . . . When the workers, organized, strong in their convictions and in singleness of purpose, take their stand in the national Association, not only as citizens but as working men, they will no longer have to fear that their hopes will be disappointed or that every revolution will waste itself on the question of political forms only to the advantage of a single class . . . The workers have special needs . . . Merely political remedies are not enough; yet revolutions will always be merely political, so long as they are entrusted to the single impulse of the other classes. The conditions of these other classes are radically different: why should they labour to provide for needs they do not themselves feel and for which there is no collective demand on the part of those who do feel them? . . . To what is due the progress made during the last ten years in social questions in France and England, if not to the workers' unions? . . . Italian workers, you will always be deceived and betrayed until you understand that before the labour element plays its part, with the rest, in bringing about political change, it must obtain citizenship in the State, which it does not possess today; and that to win this, association is indispensable . . . You have fought, so far, for the programme of the other classes: you must now draw up your own, and declare that you will fight for that alone . . . Believe in us. Whoever speaks to you in another way deceives himself or you.' 'Organization of the working-classes will affect the solution of the economic problem more than any method previously considered.' And it is curious to note how these arguments were used by Mazzini to demonstrate the necessity of class organization to certain working men who complained that 'in wishing to organize all the Italian workers in one body', Mazzini 'would perpetuate the very distinction between the classes that he declared he wanted to destroy'.

To observe how similar these ideas are to socialist theories, it is sufficient to read some of the books which in Mazzini's time dealt with social matters from the more orthodox point of view. 'It is true', wrote Silvio Pellico in the *Doveri degli uomini*, 'that in human society merit is not always adequately rewarded. Such is the world, and it is useless to hope that it will change. One can but resign oneself, cheerfully, to this necessity.

The important thing is to have merit, not to have merit that is recompensed by other men. Do everything in your power to become a useful citizen and to induce others to do likewise, and then let things go as they will. Injustice and misfortunes are to be regretted, but cannot be remedied. Do not shut yourself away from your fellow-creatures on that account.' 'The ignorant lower classes should be enlightened by ideas that will preserve them from error and exaggeration, from wild and foolish thoughts of anarchism and government by the workers; they must be taught that social inequality is a necessity.' A novel by Carcano tells the story of a young girl who works in a factory and is seduced by the manager; she is beloved by a peasant who rescues her and wants to marry her, but the girl has contracted consumption in the factory. The Almighty puts an end to this tragic situation by sending a landslide down the mountain to crush the unhappy maiden. The spectacle of so much misfortune and injustice only arouses the following mild comment on the author's part: 'Thus the Lord granted an early end to her sufferings: and in so doing it was doubtless His wish to save her from further distress and adversity. Who can question His mysterious and beneficent Will?'[1] Another example may be quoted, this time from a story by Cantù. A worthy man named Carlambrogio sees a great procession of princes, prelates and noble lords, all splendidly arrayed, and is filled with envy, but quickly reproves himself: 'Come, Carlambrogio! Stop thinking

[1] Quoted by De Sanctis, *La Letteratura Italiana nel secolo XIX*, p. 46.

of over-reaching yourself, you will only endanger your neck. Society is like a pyramid; there is room for very few at the top, and in the crowded upper ranks all jostle one another. Whoever tries to climb up from below may have a very painful fall. Lower down, on the contrary, there is elbow-room for all, and you can stretch your legs as much as you like, according to your stature.'[1] A solution of the social problem very similar to that reached by the *lazzaroni* of Naples.

Mazzini's theories, too, on the ownership of property are very close to those of socialism. The evils of existing property-rights were stated by Mazzini in 1860 to be due to four causes: 1. 'The origins of the present distribution of property lie for the most part in conquest and violence, by means of which in times long past certain peoples and classes took possession of the land and of the fruits of other men's labour.' 2. 'The profits of work that has been carried out by the landowner and the labourer are not distributed on the basis of a just division in proportion to the work done.' 3. 'Private property, conferring on its owner political and legislative rights not possessed by the worker, tends to be a monopoly of the few and inaccessible to most men.' 4. 'The system of taxation is bad, and tends to preserve wealth in the landowner and to weigh most heavily on the working-classes, making any thought of savings impossible.' These are ideas common to many socialists and democrats of the first half

[1] Quoted by De Sanctis, op. cit., p. 269. With regard to the popular conservative literature of the times, see in general the admirable observations of De Sanctis, pp. 260-78.

of the nineteenth century: the socialists, however, insisted rather on the first two, the democrats on the last. The theory that property-ownership was derived from conquest was held by Saint-Simon.[1] The eighteenth century had already explained the origin of feudal property in the same way, and Saint-Simon merely applied the theory to all landed property. In the statement, too, that one of the sources of wealth is the appropriation of 'work done by others' is the germ of Marx's theory of surplus value, which is derived from Adam Smith and Ricardo, and appears in the works of a number of other socialist writers of the first half of the century; for instance, Hodgkin had written in 1815 that capital was the product of labour, ruthlessly extorted from the worker in exchange for permission to consume a part of what he himself had produced.[2]

For property to be legitimately held, it must, according to Mazzini, be 'a sign of the amount of work that the individual has put into transforming, developing and increasing the productive forces of nature'. It is 'the visible sign of our part in the transformation of the material world', and in this sense alone is it 'a constituent element of life', 'a part of human nature', 'an eternal principle'. But 'the ways in which the ownership of property are governed are not immutable, for they must be subjected, like all other human activities, to the law of progress. Those who, finding the possession of property regulated in a certain way, declare that way

[1] Fournière, *Les théories socialistes au XIXe siècle de Babeuf à Proudhon*, Paris, Alcan, 1904, pp. 296 et seqq.

[2] Fournière, op. cit., pp. 114 et seqq.; Isambert, p. 159.

to be inviolable and resist any change in it, are therefore resisting progress'. Mazzini considered that in the present social order the system of ownership was defective, and fully concurred in the criticisms made against the individualist economic order by Fourier and all other socialists. He attributed the cause of poverty to the tyranny of capital over production, and maintained that property should be regulated by the only principle that could render it legitimate; in other words, that it should 'be produced by work'.

Guided by this rule, Mazzini rejects communism, whether in the form of assigning to every individual an equal part in the produce of labour, or in that of giving to each according to his needs. He denies that a government could be set up as 'owner, possessor, distributor of everything, land, capital, instruments of labour, produce', 'without causing an upheaval in the social order, without sterilizing production, impeding progress, destroying the liberties of the individual and binding him hand and foot in a despotic, military form of society'. He envisaged a future social order in which, while certain services such as the railways would be administered by the central government, all the rest would be the concern of free producer-consumer associations that would control capital and the land, and be based on the 'indivisibility and perpetuity of collective capital'. All the members of these would receive such remuneration as was 'adequate to the necessities of life', and the profits would be divided 'according to the quantity and quality of each man's labour'.

It is clear that in such a system, individual property, free and transferable, would not exist except in the form of what the socialists call consumer products and durable goods; and capital, in which Mazzini included not only land, but also the instruments of industrial production, becomes the common property of the co-operative associations. It is the same principle upon which the socialists founded the economic organization of what Menger called 'the democratic labour State'.[1]

The immediate reforms, therefore, that Mazzini proposed for the purpose of guiding society towards a new and better economic order, were those of free, universal education; universal suffrage, that is, 'the suppression of political privilege in property-ownership'; the improvement of communications; freedom of commerce; government credit and the concession of public works to the co-operative associations; the arming of the nation; a simplified system of justice that should be accessible to the poor; immunity from taxation for all the necessities of life; and conciliation boards to resolve disagreement between capital and labour. These reforms are more or less the same as those that figure not only in the programme of other democratic movements, but also in the minimum demands of the socialist parties; for all the democrats and socialists of the time had derived their beliefs from eighteenth-century revolutionary and humanitarian thought, and from the social theories current in the first thirty years of the nineteenth century.

[1] Menger, *Lo Stato socialista*, Turin, Roux, 1905, pp. 105-40.

8

OPPOSITION BETWEEN MAZZINI'S TEACHING AND SOCIALISM

NEVERTHELESS, Mazzini's life, especially the last twenty years of it, was a continual battle against the socialists.

The two theories differed, above all, in their approach to the problem of Italian national independence. For Mazzini, this was the aim and object of every endeavour; until it was won, the organization of the workers represented for him chiefly a means of throwing into the struggle powerful forces that so far had been inactive because wholly neglected by the liberal and conservative parties. It was, in fact, in connection with the struggle against the Austrians, in which the efforts of the upper classes had proved insufficient, that he first thought of organizing the workers. 'Oh! How disappointed I am about Milan!' he wrote on August 18th, 1834. 'Milan has always been my dream, my promised land. But corruption is there. Yet something could be done, though to attempt it we should need means and men that we do not now possess: a brotherhood of the people, I mean of those we really call the people: an anti-Austrian brotherhood, of knives and strong arms — this idea of a league of proletarians seems impracticable, yet it would not be so if we could release certain springs of action that might one day prove a danger, but are always strong in the populace: and there has not yet been war in Italy between the people and our tyrants . . . Let us speak of other things, because we cannot bring it about: I say it only to you and it must not be repeated to others, most of whom would be alarmed at the very thought.' These words envisage the possibility of what took place twenty years later, on February 6th, 1853.

It is true that *la patria*, according to Mazzini, is not an isolated organism, but one destined to form part of an international federation of all *patrie*. He goes so far as to say that in a later phase of human development the *patria* may not any longer exist.[1] But the patriotic conception was always uppermost in his mind, and he constantly affirmed that its realization was the chief task of the nineteenth century. And Mazzini had good reason for claiming that it was his own propaganda that had introduced into the vague cosmopolitanism of the old humanitarian associations 'the idea of nationhood as an end to be fulfilled in the services of Humanity itself'.[2]

Socialist theories, instead, whether they rejected the national idea outright and organized mankind into uniform *phalanstères*, like Fourier, or in federated communities, like Robert Owen, or whether they

[1] 'The idea of the *patria*, which today is sacred, will perhaps disappear some day when every man's inmost spirit will reflect the moral law of humanity.' '*La Patria*, sacred for many centuries to come.'

[2] See De Sanctis, op. cit., p. 422.

simply proclaimed the necessity of universal peace, disarmament and brotherhood between the peoples, always opposed or wholly neglected the fostering of national sentiment; they put economic questions first, and regarded national ones as a stumbling-block to the solving of the social problem.

Furthermore, it must not be forgotten that if on some, even important points, Mazzini's teaching coincided with that of socialism, the spirit animating each doctrine was always completely different. Mazzini's was a religious and moral theory, which aimed at making man a more virtuous, and through virtue, a more happy being. It was not so much poverty that he set out to destroy as the spirit of egoism and self-interest, which he regarded as the cause of poverty as of all other social evils; and he wanted to destroy it by the moral force of an education that would reveal to men the necessity for a new religious, political and economic order based on association. Socialism, on the other hand, is an economic and political system which considers as a fundamental problem to be solved that of the production and distribution of wealth, so as to increase the welfare of the proletariat; from this increase in material prosperity the disappearance, or at least the decrease, of vice and depravity must follow. While socialism springs from the philosophy of utilitarianism as both necessary and moral, Mazzini's system presupposes the philosophy of freedom and the morality of duty.

In Fourier's system, for example, it is not the economic theories that Mazzini criticizes, for he declares himself largely in agreement with them, but he asks: 'And what of God? And His law? And the mysterious force that leads us to seek it? The religions that spring from it? The future of the individual? Immortality? Genius, which is the intimation of immortality? Virtue, which shows the way to it? What do you make of all this? What do you make of that need for belief that fills our whole being and makes doubt intolerable to us? And of that part of our soul that looks always to the infinite, that longs to lose itself in the immensity of the spirit, that aspires to the unknown, the Invisible; that ever seeks their symbols in life; that penetrates the Universe as though it were no more than a veil shrouding from us the mystery of its teaching? How would you direct the great Love that embraces all humanity, those passions, so pure, so disinterested, that are nourished by misfortune and sacrifice, that ask for nothing here on earth, not even for human sympathy? What would you do with the spirit of abnegation, of sacrifice, without which friendship, love, virtue, cannot exist? Nothing? Do you believe that the uneasiness, the anxieties, the febrile agitation by which men's minds are troubled today will cease as a result of your reforms? Do you believe that for man it is only a question of regulating his existence and setting his house in order? That the void that consumes his heart is merely caused by the absence of controlled production, and that the many suicides of which you speak do not reveal more than a lack of economic equilibrium? Do you believe that great revolutions are simply the outcome of a bad industrial order? In short, do you believe that Man is nothing more than a machine for producing, or a force destined only to serve some material end? Disabuse your mind of such ideas. The void is far deeper, the needs of human nature and of the epoch in which we live are far more numerous and more spiritual than you think. Man is a being that goes ever in search of the key to a great mystery. If he mistakes the way, if something occurs to cloud his consciousness of the mission he is performing, he doubts and is unhappy. Such is our condition today. Our faith has failed us. We feel the need to love and to believe; because loving and believing constitute life. To believe in what? To love what? And in what way? This is what we all ask. Every doctrine that does not begin by giving an answer to such questions, is false; or rather, it is no doctrine.'

The main accusation that Mazzini makes against all the different schools of socialism, not excluding, and rightly, that of Saint-Simon,[1] is that they are derived from the utilitarianism of Bentham; that they make life consist simply in the search for happiness, and that by materializing the problem of life they have substituted for the progress of humanity 'the progress of humanity's *cuisine*'.[2] From this point of view, Mazzini's teaching, in departing from that of socialism, approaches that of Christian Democracy.

It is true that Mazzini recognizes the uselessness of

[1] Fournière, op. cit.; Isambert, op. cit., pp. 60, 66, 76.
[2] Mazzini is evidently thinking here of Fourier's *Gastrosophie*.

preaching moral improvement to workers brutalized by poverty. He knew well that political and economic reforms should be set on foot without delay, to improve the workers' lot and to create conditions for their moral progress. 'Take a man who in working sixteen hours a day earns scarcely enough for the bare necessities of life. He eats his potatoes and lard in a den rather than a house, then, exhausted, lies down and sleeps. His moral and physical life is that of a beast. What good are books to such a man? By what possible means can you awaken in him a soul that is so benumbed? How give him time and strength to develop his faculties if not by reducing his hours of work and increasing his wage? How turn the kind of contact he has with the well-to-do classes into one of affection, if not by changing its fundamental character?' 'We cannot calmly say to such a man: be hungry and love. We cannot insist on his educating himself when he has to work like a machine all day long to obtain a precarious subsistence; we cannot urge him to be free and pure when everything about him speaks of servitude and incites him to hatred and rebellion.' 'Your material conditions must be changed, if you are to develop morally; you need to work less and to dedicate a few hours a day to the improvement of your mind. You need wages that will enable you to put savings aside, that your minds may be relieved about the future; and above all you need to cleanse yourselves from all thought of revenge and injustice towards those who have treated you unjustly.'

Thus from the practical point of view the difference between Mazzini's teaching and that of socialism is largely one of nomenclature. Mazzini's working-man has, not the right, but the duty to safeguard his economic and political position, because the betterment of his material condition is indispensable to his moral improvement; the socialist worker has the right to better his own material conditions, and in this way also to raise himself to a higher moral level; both the one and the other, though different in approach, pursue in reality immediate aims that are identical. But this does not alter the fact that the two theories are fundamentally different, and that the propaganda of each repudiated that of the other.

Finally, the methods by which each sets out to achieve this same end of bettering the workers' lot are irreconcilable. The socialist view starts from the conception of history as a succession of class struggles: no class has ever willingly abandoned its position; indeed, those classes economically and politically in control have exploited their power by opposing any economic change in the structure of society and in the corresponding political progress of the classes that would profit from such change. In the socialist view we have reached a stage of social evolution at which, under the pressure of industrialism, property tends to assume socialized forms, with the rise of the proletariat and the disappearance of class distinctions, and consequently of the former conflicts; it is to the advantage, therefore, of the proletariat to organize itself economically and politically into a class party to hasten social change for its own benefit and to break down the political resistance of the *bourgeoisie.* Mazzini's system is based on an entirely different conception of history, which he regards as the continual progress of Association. One era does not absorb and dissolve the social elements of the preceding one, but adds new elements to them, giving place to a more perfect equilibrium of forces, a wider synthesis. Conflict is a characteristic phenomenon of a backward stage in civilization and decreases as the human race, according to the Divine plan, progresses towards moral perfection; in the next social era there will be no more conflicts whether international or social and all the elements of life will find their final equilibrium. It is our duty to hasten the coming of this future by promoting in every possible way the application of the collective principle. Class warfare, therefore, is immoral and unjust, indeed, the worst of crimes against society.

Perhaps the two theories, of the class war and of association, are both true, their error — external to themselves — consisting in the fact that each tries to exclude the other. For when they are reconciled (with Mazzini's mysticism, naturally, eliminated) there emerges the most satisfactory theory of the historical process that in the present stage of our knowledge it is possible to formulate. There are moments — when, that is, conditions favourable for production must be assured — when the interests of all or of some of the social classes constituting a nation or several nations coincide, and we then have the association of such classes or nations in pursuance of a common aim. And there are other times — when problems of distribution have to be solved — in which interests are divergent, and then there is conflict between classes or nations. Very often in the same historical period there are problems the solution of which requires the association of those very elements which are in conflict with one another over the solving of other problems; and from such involved situations is derived the usually confused and unpredictable way in which events develop. But even if Mazzini could have accepted so eclectic an explanation as this of what has happened in the past — its eclecticism being, in fact, largely apparent, since fundamentally it is only the theory of the class war deprived of its rigid over-simplification — it is certain that he would never have dreamed of accepting it in determining what must be accomplished today if we are to be set upon the right road to the future.

Mazzini who, in the political struggle against the Austrians, against the Papacy, and against the despotic rulers of Italy, unceasingly preached the necessity of insurrection, and who was not even averse to regicide, opposed any sort of violence in the field of social conflict and insisted on peaceful and gradual change.[1]

[1] It must, however, be noted that Mazzini's rejection of the use of violence in social conflicts dates only from 1848. He began by being as unrestrained as the other socialists and democrats of his time. In 1832 he believed a great political and social revolution to be imminent, and was working to hasten its coming. In 1835 he wrote: 'Arise, awake! Do you not hear a subterranean sound as of a ship breaking up in a tempest, a sound of imminent destruction? It is the old Europe that is about to fall . . . It is the young Europe arising . . . Sons of God and of Humanity,

Having heard it said that the existence of large manufacturing centres helped to determine the struggle between the proletariat and the middle classes, he expressed satisfaction that such abnormal and exaggerated industrial development did not exist in Italy, Hungary, the countries under the rule of Austria, Germany and Poland. He rarely used the word 'proletariat', preferring that of 'the people'.

This latter word has for Mazzini a number of meanings. Sometimes he uses it in referring collectively to all the classes composing a nation, 'the People one and indivisible, which knows neither caste nor privilege, neither proletariat nor aristocracy of land or finance'. At times he means all the population apart from the aristocracy: 'between the throne and the people an aristocracy is indispensable'; 'the people, the mass of townsmen and peasants', in distinction from the aristocracy and the clergy. He often distinguishes 'the middle classes', the *bourgeoisie*, from the people, making the people synonymous with the industrial working-class. At other times he employs the word in designating the artisans, in opposition to the well-to-do; 'On the one hand stands the people, on the other the privileged classes; king, nobles, rich *bourgeois* and others like them.' In general it may be said that Mazzini intends by the word *people* the middle and lower middle classes

bestir yourselves. The hour has struck.' In 1836 he wrote: 'A great social crisis in Europe becomes every day more inevitable; a crisis in which all the present powers will be smashed to pieces like glass.' In 1852, on the other hand, we find that voluntary collectivism between the workers is to replace individual paid work, 'peacefully and progressively in so far as is possible'; and in 1871 his attitude was the same.

and the tradespeople, excluding the industrial and rural proletariat. In his oft repeated formulae, 'revolutions must be made by the people for the people', and 'all for the people through action by the people', it is impossible to determine the exact meaning of the word.

The word *democracy* was one that did not fully satisfy him. 'The expression *social government* would be preferable, as indicating the idea of association, which is the life of the epoch. In the ancient world, *democracy* conveyed a sense of rebellion, sacred, but still rebellion. All such thoughts imply imperfection and are inferior to that of Unity, which will be the dogma of the future.' 'Logically speaking, the term democracy denotes war made by the people against an aristocracy based on privileges of birth, which amongst us will not exist.'

In dealing with the subject of taxation, a classical field for social conflict, Mazzini does not admit that one class should profit from the revenue of imposts which, levied upon the citizens as a whole, should be used for the benefit of all. Nowhere in his written works does he accept the idea of a progressive tax upon income. Changes in the economic order must be introduced 'without injury to others'. The workers' associations must procure capital 'without laying hands on wealth already acquired by the citizens', and since the savings of the workers themselves could not obviously provide sufficient capital to transform the social order, Mazzini expected the middle classes to facilitate working-class emancipation by providing credit for the associations and by allowing the workers meanwhile to share in the profits of their undertakings. This would represent 'an intermediate stage between the present and the future' and 'would probably provide the means for the workers to collect the small amount of capital necessary to make the associations independent'. Above all, he proposed that the Government should set up a national fund from the proceeds of the sale of Church property, the profits of the railways and other public services, communal revenue, and from a tax levied upon collateral inheritance, for the same purpose.

In Mazzini's eyes, organization of the working-class was desirable, and he did what he could to promote it, awarding it the function, first, of contributing towards the winning of national independence and then of hastening the solution of the social problem; but even in the latter field he never considered it as a weapon to be used against the capitalist class, nor did he envisage resistance or strikes as being a part of its function. Working-class organization was to be the means of forging bonds of brotherhood between the workers, of promoting their moral and intellectual progress, of vindicating their political rights, especially that of universal suffrage, and of instituting co-operative societies for the production and consumption of goods and for credit. It was above all to be the best way of making known the needs of the poorer classes to those above them in the social scale, so that the latter might provide for them. 'The whole nation', wrote Mazzini in 1842, explaining the object of such organization, 'ought to know what the workers suffer and what they demand . . . Organize yourselves, therefore, so that your distress and some indication of the necessary remedies may be made known to the Italian nation.' Thirty years later, at the Congress of Workers' Societies held in Rome in November 1871 under Mazzini's inspiration, the promotion of a general inquiry into the needs of the workers figured in the forefront of the moral, social and political aims of the organization, but no reference was made either to economic conflict or to strikes.

If, however, the higher ranks of society should fail in their duty towards the rest, what ought the lower classes to do? Mazzini never answers this most embarrassing question: such an hypothesis seems to him so pregnant with disaster that his mind shies away from the idea. It would be equivalent to casting doubt upon the existence of God, of progress, collective humanity, the divine revelation, duty, and the mission of mankind; indeed, to demolishing his whole system. It would show disbelief in the omnipotence of education. Because 'in whatever direction we turn, we always encounter the same problem: the necessity for change, for moral improvement in those who, whether from their number or their favourable position in life, have efficacious means at their disposal which are lacking to us. And the same solution always presents itself: all moral change for the better is a question of education, and all education is essentially religious'. 'The classes that today oppress you, whether voluntarily or no,' said Mazzini to the workers, 'must be made to understand their duties towards you . . . Preach Duty to those belonging to the classes above you and fulfil your own duties in so far as you may; preach virtue, sacrifice, and love; be virtuous and ready for sacrifice and love. Put your ideas and your needs courageously into words, without anger, without revengefulness and without threats; the most potent threat, if you have need of it, is firmness, not bitter words.' The upper classes, so long as they were not alarmed by immoderate demands or threats of violence, would listen, and would make provision.

If this irreconcilable opposition between Mazzini and the socialists over relations between the classes is not taken into account, it is impossible to understand his different attitude towards socialism before and after 1850.

The so-called Utopian socialists of the first half of the nineteenth century all preached the union of classes as a solution of the social problem. And socialism, which later was so often to be found in opposition to democracy, favoured, before 1850, a democratic policy inspired by a desire to improve conditions for the lower classes by means of a new system of property, which the Government and upper classes, imbued with a better moral spirit through a new form of education were to bring about. It was, in fact, often contrasted with communism, which was considered a really revolutionary heresy and a continuation of the eighteenth-century theories of Babeuf.[1]

[1] Weill, op. cit., p. 309; *Histoire du parti républicain*, pp. 320 et seqq.; Fournière, op. cit., pp. 10, 17, 306 et seqq.; Isambert, op. cit., pp. 66, 297, 371, 357. See also Martello, *Storia dell'internazionale*, Padua, Fratelli Salmin, 1873, pp. 491-2.

So long as socialism continued along these lines, Mazzini considered himself a socialist. Indeed, he was one of the first to adopt the word socialism.[1] In 1834 he wrote that 'the new movement is destined to constitute humanity, in the form of socialism'; and in 1838 he refers to 'mission, humanity, continuous progress, socialism', as being ideas of the same nature. In 1849, while criticizing adversely the utilitarian character of all the socialist schools, and contrasting them with his own plan of social reconstruction, he wrote: 'Socialism, which is an aspiration rather than a system, is only of value as a desire to substitute progressive association for the unbridled anarchy of individual rights and privileges that today clash with one another'; and he reproves Pius IX because he confuses socialism with communism, 'although the former is a philosophical rejection of the latter'. In 1850 he again deplores the fact that 'owners of property fear socialism, because they judge it by exaggerated manifestations which give a false impression of that sacred principle'. For this reason Mazzini must be included with Saint-Simon, Fourier, Leroux, Pecqueur and other humanitarians of the first half of the nineteenth century, as forerunners of modern socialism.

[1] Isambert, op. cit., p. 209, states that the first to adopt the word 'socialism' was Pierre Leroux, in an article entitled '*De l'individualisme et du socialisme*', published in the *Revue encyclopédique* in the spring of 1834; but Weill, in *L'école saint-simonienne*, p. 309, finds the word already used on Feb. 13th, 1832, in the *Globe saint-simonien*. At all events it was Leroux who, if he did not create it, put the term into circulation; and Mazzini was using it soon after. According to Holyoake, in his *History of Co-operation*, I, pp. 191, 219, the followers of Owen described themselves as *socialists* at the Manchester Congress of 1836. The word was in common use after 1840; see Menger, op. cit., p. 21.

But little by little as the proletarian movement assumed a more revolutionary character, and the word socialism became removed from the idea of a simple, co-operative form of democracy and grew to be identified with that of the class struggle — as happened during the three years from 1848 to 1851 under the impulse given by Blanqui and Marx — Mazzini became profoundly antagonistic towards this new movement with ideals differing so widely from his own. He wrote in 1851: 'We are not communists, nor levellers, nor are we opposed to the ownership of property, nor socialists in the sense given to the word by a sectarian school of thought in a neighbouring country.' And in 1852, after Louis Napoleon's *coup d'état*, the whole responsibility for which he attributed to the French socialists who had frightened the *bourgeoisie* into Caesarism, he broke with his former friends, crying, 'We must show abhorrence for the *coup d'état*, but no mercy towards the socialists.'[1] Thus began the systematic campaign against socialism which he was to wage until the end of his life.

[1] Thomas, op. cit., pp. 124-31; Mormina-Penna, *L'idea sociale di Giuseppe Mazzini e i sistemi socialisti*, Bologna, Tip. Cooperativa Azzoguidi, 1907, pp. 314 et seqq. Mazzini's bitter disputes with the French socialists and in general, his relations with the other European revolutionaries, would form the subject of an interesting study.

9

MAZZINI'S SOCIAL IDEAS AND THE RISORGIMENTO

WHILE Mazzini was preaching these theories in Italy, the men who were carrying on the struggle for national independence had to contend with the diplomatic situation resulting from the 1815 treaties, to prosecute the war against Austria, to combat the despotism of the ruling princes, supported as they were by both aristocracy and clergy, and to defy all those local interests and prejudices which were inimical to the idea of Italian unity.

No contribution towards the national effort could be expected from the peasantry and agricultural labourers, and little reliance could be placed, before 1860, in the city working classes except in urban centres of northern and central Italy. The only available forces were those of the far from numerous liberal section of the aristocracy; the industrial, commercial and professional middle class; the young intellectuals and university students; and, after 1848, a few groups of city artisans and skilled workers.[1] It was necessary for the House

[1] Before 1848 the strongest element in the *Giovine Italia* consisted of university students and young intellectuals. Although Mazzini approved the idea of forming 'two *Giovine Italia* organizations, one with student and the other with working-

of Savoy, guided by the genius of Cavour, to become associated with these forces and to appease or at least reduce the hostility of the conservative aristocracy by bringing Napoleon III into the conflict with Austria, before conditions were created in which a union of almost all forces in the nation could become possible, as happened suddenly between the armistice of Villafranca and the battle of the Volturno.

Let us suppose for a moment that the young intellectuals, the professional *petite bourgeoisie* and the upper levels of the working classes, in whom there was a glimmering of political consciousness, had not found in Mazzini's teaching a theory that, while proclaiming

class membership' (Mazzini, *Epistolario,* VI, 230; see also *Giovine Italia,* ed. Menghini, p. 121), he had no opportunity until 1840 'to study this valuable element' (Mazzini, *Scritti editi ed inediti,* Milano-Roma, Daelli, 1861-91, VI, 91). 'C'est un élément que nous avions trop négligé jusqu'ici et qui nous promet de la force', he wrote in April 1840 (*Epistolario,* IX, 85). Again, in 1843, 'time must be allowed for ideas to penetrate, little by little, from the youth of the middle classes to the people, even if only that of the towns' (Mazzini, *Scritti,* ed. Daelli, VII, 140). In 1847, 'We must confess that in 15 years we have only succeeded in arousing political passion in the young intellectuals, never in the people.' (Correnti, *Scritti scelti,* Roma, Forzani, 1891, I, 4. See Tivaroni, op. cit., pp. 111, 428-9, 478 et seqq.; 496, 508.)

From 1848 onwards, the workers began to enter the national movement, 'of their own accord and as a result of their opinions' (Bonfadini, *Mezzo secolo di patriottismo,* Milano, Treves, 1886, p. 359), accepting Mazzinian ideas. The attempt of Feb. 6th, 1853, while it produced a break between Mazzini and many middle-class patriots, was the first noteworthy sign of the entry of the workers into Mazzini's orbit: 'signs of a moral transformation in the working-classes afterwards appeared more often and more openly' (Mazzini, *Scritti,* Daelli, VIII, 227-8). According to Felice Orsini (*Memorie,* p. 127), in 1854 the Mazzinian party in Milan consisted exclusively of workers.

Afterwards the proletarian character of the Mazzinian party continued to increase, although the student element always remained (Mazzini, *Scritti,* ed. Daelli, VII, 136; XIV; *Lettres de Joseph Mazzini à Daniel Stern,* Paris, Libr. Germer, Baillière, 1873, p. 34; J. W. Mario, *Agostino Bertani,* Firenze, Barbèra, 1888, I, 267; Schak, *Giuseppe Mazzini e l'unità italiana,* Rome, Soc. ed. Laziale, 1892, p. 90; *Politica segreta italiana,* Torino, Roux e C., 1891, p. 391; Rosi, op. cit., pp. 982, 983, 992, 1000); the middle classes joined the conservative parties (Mazzini, ed. Daelli, III, XIV, XVI).

the urgency of social reform, invoked the union of all classes in winning national unity first, as the indispensable basis for all progress. If we suppose that these classes, to whom national unity alone must certainly have appeared inadequate as a remedy for all their ills, had not had a theory to cling to, which, while exalting patriotic sentiment, also satisfied their still somewhat confused longing for a better social order, we should be forced to admit that in all probability the void left by Mazzini's teaching and by his ideas on association would have been filled by socialism and class warfare. Much strength would thereby have been lost to the national movement: many among those who fought and died for a patriotic and democratic ideal in which national unity was regarded as the way to a solution of the social problem, would have rejected the patriotic ideal alone, as insufficient; instead, they would have dedicated themselves to speeding up and directing the first struggles between *bourgeoisie* and proletariat. They would have aroused suspicion and alarm in the middle classes; they would have isolated those in the national movement; and moreover they would have turned the *bourgeoisie* once more towards absolutist ideas, since in the renewal of Italian national life the middle classes sought not the destruction of private property, but the possibility of safeguarding and augmenting it. The harm done would have been all the greater in proportion to the many anarchical and ultra-revolutionary varieties of socialism current in Europe between 1850 and 1870.

Mazzini was well aware of the danger. In 1838, on hearing that a secret society had been formed with the programme of abolishing both private property and religion, he wrote: 'Wretched and insensate fools! If Metternich himself had drawn up the programme of the organization, he could have done no better.' He often deplored the fact that communist theories 'produced the double evil of discouraging the activities of many true friends of the people and of using up the energies of numerous well-intentioned but deluded workers' on impossible projects, thus distracting them from creating 'a nation and a name' for themselves. He regretted that communism was 'an incitement to sterile discord, a pretext for unmerited accusations that obstruct the progress of democracy', and grieved that 'the middle classes had become less forward in the way of action and sacrifice since the people had shown signs of having a life of their own'. He constantly affirmed the necessity of reciprocal trust, of harmony between all those who formed the Nation, in order that Italy might 'arise in all the splendour of popular faith'.[1]

Had such teaching emanated simply from the conservative element in the country, it would certainly have been regarded with suspicion by the young intellectuals and the workers, and might well have had the opposite effect from that intended. Coming, however, as it did, from a man whom all were accustomed to consider an

[1] The necessity for all classes to unite against the foreigner was stressed also by the moderate parties. See Balbo, *Speranze d'Italia*, pp. 346 et seqq.; D'Azeglio, *Scritti politici e letterari*, I, pp. 179, 182, 183, 184, 445; Bianchi, *Storia documentata della diplomazia europa*, IV, 258.

inveterate revolutionary, who during his whole life had suffered persecution at the hands of the government, it could not but make a deep impression;[1] and for a long time it served as a barrier to the spread of communist ideas, and facilitated the concentration of all forces on what was the necessity of the moment: united action against the enemies within and without the country, for the conquest of national independence.

Once this was achieved, the new political situation gave rise to nothing resembling that concord of all classes from which Mazzini expected the solution of the social problem to be evolved. Industrialism, which he believed to be an anomaly appertaining to England and France, quickly developed in Italy. The national fund which was to provide capital for the workers' associations never materialized; Church property was squandered, communal property almost everywhere seized upon, the railways handed over to private companies; the whole basis for Mazzini's humanitarian mission was lacking. Inquiries into agrarian conditions revealed appalling distress, without arousing any resolute action to remedy it; while the system of taxation was so contrived as to promote a brutal class war of the strong against the weak. Education for the people was the last thing to interest the new ruling classes. Thus, the new Italy found herself subjected to a rapacious oligarchy intent upon exploiting its political position to its own advantage.

[1] This is an acute observation which Martello, in his *Storia della Internazionale*, p. 430, reproduces from a French pamphlet of 1871.

Mazzini's social theories then revealed themselves as a generous but Utopian dream; they showed the workers the goal, but forbade them to take the only way that led to it. And while the newcomers of the middle classes, satisfied with national unity, gave their allegiance to the monarchy, those of the lower classes and the young intellectuals went over into the ranks of socialism. Mazzini's social system, from the practical point of view, no longer corresponded with prevailing social and political realities. It slowly faded away, as the master's nearest disciples died or left him.

But in the meantime, the unification of Italy had been achieved. The minimum programme that Mazzini had imposed on the Italian political parties was realized.

And his other theories? Mazzini's attempt to confine art to the service of a social and political mission was obviously a mistaken one; yet in its time it served as a reminder to some of the best Italians that in dedicating themselves to their art, they had no right to neglect their duties to their country: and it was thus that Mameli's hymn was born. There must be few indeed today who would repeat with Mazzini that God had assigned to Rome and to Italy the mission of initiating a new era in the history of civilization; but under the rule of the foreigner, this illusion aroused in many Italian hearts an overwhelming urge to create the unity of their country. The Republic was evidently not included in God's plan, at any rate for many years to come; but fear of it acted as a goad to the House of

Savoy, urging them ever forward on the way of political unity, and thus bringing national interests into line with their own.

As to Mazzini's religious faith, how many among us would now accept it? Nevertheless, we should be greatly mistaken were we to regard with the same indifference the would-be theological and scholastic elements in his creed and the spiritual vigour from which it sprang and which kept it unimpaired through half a century of conflict and adversity. Such confusion of thought would prevent our understanding the irresistible influence that Mazzini has, even today, on all who approach him, despite the fact that many perishable elements in his teaching have no longer any meaning for us. Duty placed in the forefront of life, self-sacrifice upheld as the only virtue, social and international solidarity preached as the moral faith of humanity: these principles — which every man who wishes to impose his own will over others should take as his prop and stay, if he wishes to do good, or to persuade himself that such is his intention — have never been more sincerely or more forcefully affirmed than by Mazzini: affirmed not in a system of abstract ideas, but — what is much more important — in the activity and anguish of his daily life.

Malwida von Meysenbug quotes a comment of Nietzsche's upon Mazzini which shows the power possessed by this ascetic figure, stricken but unbowed, of evoking warm admiration even in those who might seem little likely to be in sympathy with him.

'Nietzsche said that, of all fine lives, he envied most Mazzini's: that absolute concentration upon a single idea which becomes as it were a flame consuming all that is personal in life. The poet turns his inner urge to action into the characters he creates, and so projects doing and suffering outside himself. Mazzini expressed his in his own life, which was the continual manifestation in word and deed, of a most noble spirit. He was himself the tragic protagonist who accepts grievous suffering in order to bring about fulfilment of the ideal.'[1]

This suffering was accepted by Mazzini because he had a heroic vision of the world, of history and of life; because he thought that, in toiling and enduring, he could contribute towards a great work of universal equity; and because he was convinced that his efforts were not confined to their immediate ends, but that every beat of his heart responded to a rhythm of eternal and inviolable justice.

In this 'sense of the universal' lies the secret of the powerful fascination which Mazzini exerted during his life-time, and which his writings still exert in many, often unexpected, quarters. Mazzini was a man who did not live for himself. His desire was to live and to suffer for all men; in so doing he lived and suffered for us too. For this reason we feel we can always turn to him — even if our opinions now differ wholly from his — as to a brother, or a father; ever certain of finding in him inspiration and comfort: inspiration in our hours of weariness, and comfort in defeat.

[1] Malwida von Meysenbug, *Der Lebensabend einer Idealisten*, Berlin, Schuster & Loeffler, 1905.